T0289612

THE
NO-CODE
STARTUP

The complete guide to building apps without code

EMMA REILLY

First published in Great Britain by Practical Inspiration Publishing, 2024

ISBN 9781788605069 (PB print)
      9781788605786 (HB print)
      9781788605083 (epub)
      9781788605076 (mobi)

Want to bulk-buy copies of this book for your team and colleagues? We can customize the content and co-brand *The No-Code Startup* to suit your business's needs.

Please email info@practicalinspiration.com for more details.

Practical Inspiration
Publishing

Dedication

To my parents, Susan and Kevin, my sister Nic and my
nephew William. You are my everything. This book is
possible because of everything you did for me.

M'Suze, you are my second home and my inspiration.

Caz. My world and my rock. You got me through it.
I love you.

Contents

Preface

My previous startup spent a whopping £50,000 to create a Minimum Viable Product (MVP). We partnered with a top-tier agency and a standout developer, resulting in an impressive web application. However, I distinctly remember the sinking feeling as I played with our new product, realizing, 'This just won't resonate with our target customers'.

Ironically, I was unaware of the concept of no-code at that time, despite having used several no-code tools over the past decade. To me, these were just handy utilities for website building or data storage. Little did I know I could integrate these tools to construct something truly remarkable. While no-code platforms like Bubble, Glide, and Airtable were still budding, a diligent exploration could have allowed me to build a comparable product to our expensive MVP at a fraction of the cost – around £700. That would have been a much easier pill to swallow if our product didn't meet our customers' expectations.

Fast forward a few years, and my professional and personal interest in product development has led me to plunge headfirst into the no-code universe. I've created a wide array of products – a marketplace, an epilepsy tracker, a publishing platform, and a community. While not all were successful, the exhilarating journey of ideation, experimentation, and testing the limits of available tools has been truly rewarding.

This book is dedicated to anyone who's ever had an idea flicker at the back of their mind but didn't know how to bring it to life. It's for those who attempted to launch a startup but stumbled at the first hurdle. It's for professionals from all walks of life – designers, bankers, sales directors, accountants, doctors, caregivers, and everyone in between.

To me, no-code transcends the realm of software. It is a transformative mindset that can be applied to every facet of your business – from marketing to team management. This playbook begins at the ideation stage, offering a step-by-step process to transform your concept into a lean, no-code startup. While it's unrealistic to detail every feature and update of every no-code tool – given the rapid pace of developments – the fundamental principles of product building remain unchanged. From designing wireframes using tools like Figma to creating a relational database in Airtable, this guide escorts you through everything you need to know from day one to the launch date. It provides a roadmap for the types of no-code tools to use and the frameworks to follow.

Recently, I put these principles into practice, launching a private members club called Willo.Social using the exact playbook detailed in this book. By the time you finish this guide, I hope you will be well on your way to becoming a successful no-code startup founder yourself.

When I'm learning new no-code tools or how to build a specific feature, I like to follow step-by-step tutorials. Sometimes it's helpful to see how other builders have solved a particular problem so you can apply it to your own app. That is why I've collected some of my favourite 'how-to guides' for you to try. Check out my website at https://nocodestartup.co for the very best tools and resources. Now, let's get cracking on your first no-code project!

1

Introduction

The old days of tech startups

Step back to the early days of app development, an era characterized by risk-taking and the potential for great rewards. Those who ventured down this path were like modern-day alchemists, overflowing with courage and creativity and fueled by the energy of caffeine. These tech-savvy pioneers, often armed with a background in Computer Science, breathed life into lines of code, skillfully constructing intricate apps using sophisticated programming languages like Java, C++, and Python.

Building an app back then was like constructing a skyscraper. Frameworks like .NET, Ruby on Rails, and Django served as the scaffolding, but the developers still had to lay every brick, or in this case, write every line of code, to create functionalities.

Imagine being a non-technical founder in this landscape. Your head was filled with revolutionary ideas, yet you lacked the technical know-how to bring them to life. Your options were limited: either dive into the deep end and learn to code, hire a developer (an expensive affair), or find a tech-savvy co-founder. The lack of a developer was a significant barrier, often halting the progress of your digital dream.

No-code tools did exist but were rudimentary, limited, and not particularly user-friendly. Tools like Dreamweaver and FrontPage offered a glimpse of what was possible, but they lacked the flexibility and power of modern no-code tools. As a result, the art of creating an app was mainly confined to those who could navigate the intricate world of code.

Look at some of the tech giants we're familiar with today. Facebook, for instance, was the brainchild of Mark Zuckerberg, a computer science student who crafted the initial version of the social networking site from his Harvard dorm room. MySpace, another significant player in the early social media scene, was built using ColdFusion, a scripting language renowned for its complexity. Google, too, was born out of the coding prowess of Larry Page and Sergey Brin, two PhD students at Stanford who used complex mathematical algorithms to create the search engine we now use daily.

The early days of app development were characterized by high barriers to entry, and the time to launch was often lengthy. Without the widespread adoption of agile and lean methodologies, the development process often followed a linear model. It was not uncommon for apps to take several months, or even years, to go from conception to launch.

However, the early 2000s also saw the emergence of no-code tools that began to democratize the digital landscape. WordPress, launched in 2003, enabled people to build websites without coding. TechCrunch, one of the most influential tech blogs today, was built using WordPress, proving that success was attainable even without in-depth coding expertise.

Despite these advancements, the functionality of early no-code tools was limited, and customizing these platforms often required coding skills. While they provided a steppingstone, they were not the complete solution that today's no-code tools are.

Today, we're witnessing a no-code revolution. Modern no-code platforms have evolved into powerful tools that enable anyone with an idea to develop complex apps without writing a single line of code. The development process has become faster, leaner, and more inclusive, opening the digital gold rush to a broader range of participants.

As we journey through this book, we will delve deeper into this revolution, exploring how no-code tools are disrupting traditional app development and enabling a new generation of entrepreneurs to turn their ideas into reality. Whether you're a coding expert or a non-tech founder, join us as we traverse the fascinating world of no-code, a world where your digital dream is only a few clicks away.

The new world of no-code

From the outset, the journey of building an app or starting a digital business may seem daunting, especially if your skills don't include writing complex code. But this should no longer be a hurdle that stops you. The landscape has dramatically changed since the early 2000s as no-code tools have evolved and matured. They've not just simplified the process of building digital products but have also significantly reduced the time and cost involved.

If you're wondering about the power of no-code, take a look at Bubble, a platform that has empowered thousands of entrepreneurs to build software without any coding. Or consider the success of Adalo, an intuitive platform that allows anyone to create their own apps, with a range of features and design options that would have required a dedicated development team just a few years ago.

Startups and businesses that once would have spent months searching for a technical co-founder or outsourcing their projects to expensive agencies can now prototype, build, and even launch their own products. They can validate their ideas faster and cheaper than ever before, reducing risk and increasing the potential for success.

But it's not just about startups. The no-code movement is also empowering individuals, freelancers, and small businesses to create custom solutions tailored to their unique needs. From automating repetitive tasks to building personalized customer experiences, no-code tools are democratizing access to technology and innovation.

So, if you've ever had a brilliant idea for an app but shelved it because you didn't know how to code or couldn't afford a developer, it's time to dust it off and bring it to life. With the power of no-code, the only limit is your imagination. Whether you're looking to create a side hustle, grow your business, or launch the next big thing, no-code tools can help you get there.

We stand on the cusp of a new era in digital creation, where anyone can be a maker, where ideas don't have to be confined to the minds of their creators but can take form and shape in the digital world. As we embark on this journey through the world of no-code, remember this isn't just about learning how to use new tools. It's about embracing a new mindset, a new way of thinking and creating, one that empowers you to make your mark in the digital universe.

What is no-code/low-code?

In the world of technology, 'no-code' and 'low-code' have become some of the most exciting buzzwords. These terms refer to a new generation of tools that allow anyone, regardless of technical skill, to build digital products. We're going to delve deeper into what these terms mean, their origins, and the transformative power they wield in the digital world.

Let's start with the basics. 'No-code' is a term used to describe platforms that allow users to build software without writing a single line of code. Instead of typing out complex syntax and algorithms, these tools use a visual interface where users can drag and drop elements to design and build their apps.

In the early days of digital creation, coding was the only way to build software. This was a highly specialized skill, mastered only by a select few. Those who didn't have coding skills often found themselves locked out of the digital creation process. As a digital product designer myself, I felt this frustration. I found myself teetering on the edge of the digital world, able to envision products but not equipped with the tools to bring them to life.

My first encounter with a 'no-code' tool was with WordPress. In its simplest form, WordPress is a tool for building websites. But with an array of plugins, it offered me the ability to add functionalities far beyond a basic website. I could build e-commerce platforms, interactive portfolios, social media networks, and more. I even created a family recipe database for personal use.

The beauty of WordPress was that it allowed me to create complex digital products without knowing how to code. As a designer, this opened new business avenues for me. I could now offer web design services, expanding my portfolio and my market reach.

Yet, while WordPress was a godsend, it was still somewhat limiting. Certain complex functionalities were out of reach, and I had to rely on available plugins for any additional features. For example, back in 2003, while studying film production, I dreamt of a platform where students and filmmakers could upload and share their videos. However, without coding skills and being a cash-strapped student, I couldn't bring this idea to life. In 2005, YouTube was launched by a designer and two computer scientists, making my idea a reality but also showing me the limitations of no-code tools at the time.

Fast forward to today, and the landscape of no-code has dramatically evolved. New platforms have emerged, each offering more complex functionalities and greater customization. From Webflow for web design to Bubble for full-stack app development, the possibilities seem endless. Now, non-technical founders can build software products, automate workflows, and even implement AI capabilities, all without writing a single line of code.

You may have also come across something called a 'low-code' platform. These tools still require some coding, but much less than traditional programming. They typically feature a visual interface for design and allow users to add custom code for more advanced functionalities.

Low-code platforms, like OutSystems or Mendix, are trendy in enterprise settings, where they allow developers to build software faster and more efficiently. They offer the flexibility of custom coding with the efficiency of no-code, a perfect balance for many businesses.

What no-code means for today's entrepreneurs

The rise of no-code and low-code is more than just a technological advancement; it's a paradigm shift. For decades, software development was a gated community accessible only to those who spoke the language of code. Today, that gate is wide open. Anyone with an idea and determination can build software, launch a startup, or digitize their business.

This democratization of software development is reshaping the tech industry. It's breaking down barriers, levelling the playing field, and fostering a more diverse and inclusive digital ecosystem. The tech giants of tomorrow might not be founded by coding savants but by individuals who used no-code or low-code platforms to bring their visions to life. We're seeing this transformation unfold in real-time. Take Tara Reed, who built Kollecto, an art recommendation app using no-code tools. Or Vlad Magdalin, a former animator who created Webflow, a no-code platform, which is now valued at over \$2.1 billion.

The evolution of no-code and low-code is also changing the dynamics of team building within startups. Traditionally, a tech startup's first hire was often a developer or a Chief Technology Officer. Now, with no-code and low-code tools, founders can validate their ideas and build MVPs without hiring a technical team right away. This shifts the early focus from development to problem-solving and market fit, a crucial advantage in the dynamic world of startups.

One crucial point to note, though, is that no-code and low-code tools aren't here to replace developers or make coding obsolete. Instead, they are tools that make technology more accessible and foster collaboration. Developers are still needed to handle complex functionalities, security, and scalability, especially as a product grows.

The future of no-code and low-code platforms is teeming with potential, heralding a vibrant and inclusive digital age. As these tools evolve, they pave the way for groundbreaking startups, reshape traditional sectors, and foster a diverse tech landscape. Recalling my own endeavours, I often muse how my aspirations in film production, specifically my concept for a video-sharing platform, could have flourished with today's advancements. However, the essence of this digital renaissance lies in its accessibility; it's not merely about tools but about erasing barriers, fostering innovation, and embracing diversity. Whether one is a designer, a filmmaker, or an innovator with a dream, the digital frontier is now open for all to mould and venture into.

And remember, in this exciting no-code and low-code era, the only limit to what you can build is your imagination.

The limitations of no-code

No-code and low-code platforms have indeed revolutionized the tech space. By bringing the power of application development into the hands of non-technical entrepreneurs, they've allowed ideas to grow and flourish in unprecedented ways. However, as fantastic as these tools are, they aren't a magic wand. There are certain considerations and limitations that one must keep in mind while venturing into this space.

The key lies in understanding your business needs and the scope of your project and creating a plan to mitigate any potential issues.

To begin, let's talk about the creative constraints. No-code platforms, by nature, are often template-driven. They provide a set of pre-defined functions and features that you can use to build your app. This is great for getting an MVP up and running quickly. However, when it comes to implementing unique features or custom design elements, these platforms can sometimes fall short. They might not offer the level of customization you require to fully express your vision.

Take WordPress, for instance, a platform I've been familiar with for a long time. It offers an ocean of plugins that you can utilize to enhance your website's capabilities. But every plugin you add increases complexity and potentially slows down your website, and some may not work together at all. More than once, I've found myself wrestling with plugins that refused to play nice with one another.

Cost is another consideration. Many no-code platforms follow a subscription-based pricing model. This could range from a few pounds to several hundreds of pounds per month, depending on the features you need. While these costs are typically much lower than hiring a full-time developer, they can add up over time, especially if you need to connect multiple platforms together. For instance, in the early days of my no-code journey, I was using three different platforms to create my recruitment app. The cost of each tool was reasonable on its own, but combined, they amounted to a substantial monthly fee.

Something to really consider when you're building your no-code app is that you will likely need to connect different no-code tools together. While each tool might excel in its area, very few can do everything. Therefore, you might end up using one tool for your database, another for your front-end, and yet another for automations. While this is feasible, it does increase complexity and requires a higher learning curve.

This brings us to another limitation – the learning curve. Despite being easier than learning to code, mastering no-code tools still requires time and effort. Every tool has its quirks and unique ways of doing things. The more complex your app, the steeper the learning curve.

Scalability is another factor to consider. As your user base grows, can the no-code platform you've chosen handle the increased load? This is a critical point to ponder upon. My experience with a no-code tool that required frequent module refreshes each time there was an update was a wake-up call.

A crucial dependency to consider is the no-code platform itself. If it goes down, so does your app. If they decide to hike their prices or change their policy, you're at their mercy. Moreover, you're relying on the vendor for maintaining and optimizing security, which can be a concern, particularly if you collect users' personal data. Your chosen platform is essentially your partner. Therefore, it's crucial to evaluate vendors not just on their current offerings but also their roadmap, their customer service, and their financial stability. You don't want to build your application on a platform only to have the vendor shut down or pivot away from the no-code space.

Despite these limitations, with adequate planning and a clear understanding of your requirements, many of these challenges can be mitigated. If your app is likely to scale rapidly, considering a more scalable solution from the get-go, like Bubble or Flutterflow, could save you a world of pain later. If high functionality is a requirement, then low-code options that allow for custom code might be worth exploring. If you plan to handle large amounts of data, understanding the storage limitations and pricing model of your chosen platform is critical.

Though you are dependent on third-party software and the mistakes and changes they may bring, the future of no-code and low-code is bright, with the platforms evolving rapidly. More and more features and capabilities are being added regularly, shrinking the gap between what is possible with traditional coding and these platforms. For instance, Bubble, a popular no-code tool, allows users to build complex applications with custom workflows, integrations, and even a bit of code when necessary.

In my own journey, I've found no-code and low-code tools to be empowering. They've allowed me to bring my ideas to life without being hindered by the lack of coding skills. However, I've also learned that understanding these tools, their capabilities, and their limitations is crucial to their successful application.

In conclusion, the no-code and low-code movements are democratizing the app development space, making it possible for more people to bring their ideas to life. But as with any technology, these tools are not without their limitations. By understanding these limitations and planning for them, you can take full advantage of these tools while minimizing potential pitfalls. You're entering the market at a wonderful time, where you, as a no-code founder, are shaping how these tools will grow in the future.

Avoid the mistakes of my own failed startup

In the world of startups, the road to success is littered with lessons, some of them learned the hard way. Reflecting on my journey, I remember how my team and I tried to tackle the pervasive issue of mental health care in our communities. Our aim was noble; we wanted to make mental health support smarter and more personalized, using big data gleaned from people who had undergone similar experiences. However, our approach was somewhat flawed.

Our first misstep was the failure to scope our problem accurately. We wanted to help everyone, and in our passion for creating change, we overextended ourselves. Trying to be everything to everyone meant we spread ourselves thin and ended up building something that didn't satisfy anyone fully.

We should have treated our problem like a mountain, tackling it one trail at a time. Each trail would be a step forward, a step deeper into understanding our users, and a step closer to a solution. Instead, we tried to scale the mountain in a single day, and we ended up lost in the wilderness.

In hindsight, our research was impeccable; we read medical papers, conducted surveys, and consulted with experts. But the missing piece was the end user. We didn't speak to enough of them. This was a crucial mistake that significantly impacted our final product. We were fortunate to have a large company willing to pay us to test our product with their staff. However, our user pool was narrow and biased towards a single working culture. We also missed a crucial point: our users were not our customers. The HR Director, who would purchase our product, was our customer. We should have focused more on solving their problems, which in turn would have helped us to build a better product. Our journey taught me a valuable lesson: a strong user-centric approach is essential for any product, especially in the startup world.

Another major mistake that we made was that we didn't drill down into what should have been the key features of our app. In part, this was because we won a significant grant that gave us a development runway of 18 months – far too long for an MVP. We worked alongside an incredible agency, and it was exciting to see the hundreds of pages they'd created. There were mood trackers, user profiles, courses, mental health action plans, SOS buttons... It looked fantastic, but it was too bloated for a new, untested app.

As a team, we were also pretty useless. We spent too much time networking and building our brand rather than building our product. Our goals and beliefs were not aligned, and that had a detrimental impact on what we were trying to achieve.

It wasn't until the business ended that I could see how no-code could have given us the answers we needed in no more than a few months. Building quickly, cheaply, and alongside our potential customers would have meant that we could have saved years of heartache and stress. However, it wasn't all in vain. It was a learning experience that shaped me as an entrepreneur. It taught me the importance of a user-centric approach, the pitfalls of over-scoping problems, and the value of rapid prototyping. And more importantly, it reinforced the importance of understanding the customer's needs – and how the customer and the user might be different!

These lessons, learned the hard way, have informed my subsequent entrepreneurial journeys. They've made me a more informed, more strategic, and more empathetic founder. And if my story can help other entrepreneurs avoid these pitfalls and navigate their startup journey more smoothly, then every misstep and stumble will have been worth it.

One particular anecdote that stands out in my memory is the development of a 'smaller' MVP. Because we realized 18 months was too long to wait for an all singing, all dancing MVP, we would create a simpler version for the web. We worked with a developer, investing nearly £50,000 and dedicating 8–12 weeks of our time. The developer did a fantastic job, but the end result was a letdown. The product had some impressive functionality, but it failed to deliver where it mattered the most: user onboarding and problem-solving.

This experience was a wake-up call. It made me realize that cool features and impressive functionality mean nothing if your product doesn't resonate with its users. We had spent a significant amount of money and time building a product that didn't fully meet our users' needs. This was a hard pill to swallow, but it was a valuable lesson in the importance of user-centric design and development.

It's easy to let the excitement and passion of building a startup cloud your judgment, but it's crucial to stay grounded and focused. Use the tools at your disposal, whether it's no-code platforms for rapid prototyping, user interviews for deeper insights, or customer feedback to refine your product.

How to use this book

This book aims to become your trusted companion on the exciting journey of building a startup using no-code tools. We've taken a small stroll down memory lane, reminiscing about the tech-startup landscape, the evolution of no-code/low-code, some of the pros and cons of using no-code and the lessons I've personally learned as a founder. As we pivot to the practical part of this journey, it's essential to understand how to navigate this book effectively.

What awaits you in the upcoming chapters is a comprehensive playbook that will guide you through the principles of building a startup using no-code. It's designed to be more than just an informational guide. Instead, it aims to be an interactive learning experience that will teach you how to leverage no-code tools to take your idea from concept to reality.

No-code is an ever-evolving landscape. New tools and functionalities are being introduced all the time, and the best way to keep up is by staying focused on the underlying principles that drive successful implementation. That's why this book doesn't delve into how to build individual programs with specific no-code tools. Rather, it focuses on building a strong foundation and understanding of the basics of no-code, allowing you to adapt and thrive as the no-code world continues to evolve.

One unique feature of this book is its practical tasks. After each conceptual discussion, you'll find tasks that will challenge you to apply what you've learned. These tasks are designed to simulate real-world problems that startup founders face, pushing them to think critically and creatively to find solutions using no-code tools. These exercises will immerse you in the world of no-code, helping you develop practical skills and understand the principles of no-code.

Additionally, we recognize the power of learning from others. That's why we've included interviews with founders who have successfully built startups using no-code. These founders have generously shared their journeys, including their triumphs, challenges, and insights, providing you with invaluable real-world perspectives.

The reference material in this book is another crucial aspect to highlight. It includes a comprehensive list of no-code tools and resources, along with their descriptions and use cases. These references will serve as a handy guide as you embark on your no-code journey, helping you choose the right tools and resources that align with your startup's needs.

One of the key strengths I bring to this book is my experience as a startup founder. I've weathered the storms of building a startup, navigated countless challenges, and learned many lessons along the way. Throughout this book, I'll be sharing anecdotes from my journey, illustrating practical examples of how to overcome obstacles, pivot ideas, find users for testing, and more.

Moreover, we'll delve into resources beyond just no-code tools. We'll explore how to find and utilize additional tools such as graphics, photos, and copy for free. After all, building a startup is about more than just coding. It's about creating an engaging and meaningful user experience, and these resources play a significant role in that process.

In summary, this book is designed to be your all-in-one guide to navigating the world of no-code startup building. Whether you're a seasoned entrepreneur or just starting, this book will equip you with the knowledge, skills, and resources you need to build your startup using no-code tools. Remember, this journey is about learning, growing, and enjoying the process.

2

Discovery and ideation

Finding a problem to solve

We've all heard of Facebook, the stratospheric social network that has fingers in many technical pies. In the early days, it started out as a simple platform for Harvard students to connect and interact with each other before spreading to other universities and eventually to the general public. Facebook's founders identified a problem: people's desire to stay connected with their peers, even when physically separated. And they built a solution that resonated with millions around the world.

Similarly, PayPal, the global online payments system, addressed the problem of making secure, swift, and simple financial transactions over the Internet. They recognized a need, particularly in the era of burgeoning e-commerce, and developed a platform that revolutionized the way we conduct online transactions.

Etsy, on the other hand, gave crafters and artisans a solution to sell their creations to a global audience. It offered a platform for independent creators to reach a global audience, providing an easy-to-use, affordable online storefront that was previously inaccessible to many. Etsy saw a gap in the market and filled it with a solution that catered to a niche yet sizeable user base.

As these examples illustrate, every successful startup begins with a problem that needs solving. And these problems can be found anywhere – in our daily lives, in our interactions with others, and even in our personal experiences. In my case, living with a chronic pain condition exposed me to challenges I hadn't considered before. It gave me a unique perspective on the issues faced by individuals like me, prompting me to create a solution that could make their lives a little easier.

Identifying a compelling problem that needs a solution is the first and arguably most crucial step to creating a successful startup. One of the top reasons why most businesses are unsuccessful is because the founders fail to get product-market fit. That is, they've built something that people just don't want or need. Finding a problem is an art form and not just a mere exercise of picking an idea from a hat. It can take time and lots of patience. It is also important to remember from the outset that your initial problem will evolve as you get feedback from your customers. We'll deal more with that later in the book, but for now, you need to go out and find that spark.

Many of the ideas I've had over the years have stemmed from observing myself, my family, and my networks. How many times do you hear someone stating, 'Oh, I wish it did this', or 'my life would be so much easier if this happened'. Those are the clues that I try to pay attention to. Sometimes, I will encounter something that frustrates me so much that I think about how I would do it better. My startup, Willo. Social began with a very personal frustrating experience. As someone with a long-term health condition, I spent much of my covid lockdown trying to find a suitable online fitness class that would cater for my needs. It was a difficult process, and after seeing many other similar women complain about their quarantine weight gain, I thought that this was a problem to solve. At this point, I could have quite easily built a website, found a fitness expert that knew something about women's health conditions and then paid a lot of money to advertise classes on Facebook. But I also knew that could be a big waste of time. Instead, I reached out to some of these women online and found that they either had a gym membership or they were just not that interested in doing online fitness. The market was already flooded as it was, and at the time, they'd been bombarded with ads for 'female weight loss'. I realized their appetite for this app might be a bit sluggish.

During these interviews, however, I'd picked up on a fair number of people talking about cancelling plans with friends or feeling quite isolated because of their condition. Whilst researching one problem, I found another!

Finding the right problem is not a task to be rushed. It's a discovery process requiring an open mind and a keen ear. I recently asked a number of entrepreneurs how they find problems to solve. Many of them talked about finding problems in their own job, such as having to do repetitive admin tasks or not being able to find certain key metrics easily. Some said they liked to read online blogs or posts on Linkedin as it helped to spark ideas. One entrepreneur even admitted to using AI-generation tools like GPT to brainstorm problems that he could investigate more. What everyone did agree on was that talking to people and being curious was the best way to seek out problems and ideas.

One tool that became an integral part of my problem-hunting process was an idea notebook. This notebook became my constant companion, a place to capture every spark of inspiration or problem I encountered. Every conversation, every observation, every thought found a home in those pages. As an 'ideas person', my mind was always buzzing with new concepts and possibilities. However, it's easy to get overwhelmed with too many ideas. That's where the notebook came in handy. It helped me keep track of my thoughts and stay focused on the problem at hand.

One of the key elements in my journey was reaching out to other entrepreneurs, seeking their advice and feedback. Many local libraries and business-support centres offer free mentorship programs, providing invaluable guidance and perspective. As a solo founder, it was important to me to get feedback on my ideas outside of my normal customer discovery sessions. Gaining constructive critique of what you're doing actually makes your eventual product even better. These conversations were not only enlightening but also inspiring. They reminded me that every problem is an opportunity to make a difference.

In the end, the problem you choose to solve should not only be significant but also resonate with you personally. After all, you'll be spending a considerable amount of time with it. In my case, the challenges faced by individuals with chronic health conditions were close to my heart, and my passion for the issue fuelled my drive to find a solution.

Problem hunting is a delicate dance of curiosity, empathy, and persistence. It's about identifying who is affected, understanding the nature of the problem, and figuring out how it's currently being addressed. It's about listening to people's stories, analyzing trends, and making data-driven decisions. But most importantly, it's about being committed to creating a positive change in people's lives. Because in the end, the most successful startups are not just businesses; they're solutions to real-world problems.

When hunting for problems, it's essential to be objective and unbiased, even if it's something you yourself have experienced. You are just one person, so it's important to take a step back and find out if this is bigger than just you. It's incredibly easy to get attached to an idea and start seeing everything through that lens. However, such a narrow view can lead to misguided solutions. In my conversations with potential users for my new startup, now called Willo.Social, I made it a point to ask open-ended, unbiased questions. Instead of leading with, 'I'm building this community for people with chronic health conditions; what do you think?', I asked, 'When was the last time you couldn't attend something you really wanted to attend?' and 'What stopped you from going?' This approach elicited honest, unfiltered responses that helped me understand the real issues they faced.

Creating your solution: Crazy 8 framework

After you've done all of your problem research, the next step is to start ideating on how to solve that problem. There is no one-size-fits-all approach to this process. Sometimes, the solution might be instinctively apparent, as it was in my case with Willo.Social. However, there are times when you might need to brainstorm multiple solutions to generate the best idea. And then, there are those times when you're grappling with a creative block and need a little help in propelling your thoughts forward.

There are many different ways to generate ideas, and several frameworks can assist you in this endeavour. Brainstorming sessions, mind maps, and SWOT analyses are common techniques, each with its strengths and weaknesses. But among all of these, my personal favourite is the Crazy 8s framework.

The Crazy 8s framework is a fast-paced ideation technique that originated in the hallowed halls of Google Ventures. It's designed to stimulate rapid idea generation and overcome creative roadblocks. The name 'Crazy 8s' comes from the practice of folding a sheet of paper into eight sections and spending a minute sketching an idea in each section, thus generating eight ideas in eight minutes.

This exercise is very versatile. You can do it on your own or with a team. You can even rope in your trusted friends and family to help but be careful about intellectual property ownership. Remember, the goal is to create a variety of ideas, not to produce the perfect solution in one go. The aim is to free your mind and let the ideas flow.

Now, let's apply this concept to a simple problem: 'Startup founders can't afford to hire much-needed team members to help their business grow'. Here's how we're going to use the Crazy 8 framework to generate some ideas to solve this problem:

Step 1: Preparation

Get a sheet of paper and fold it so that it has eight sections. You might want to set a timer for eight minutes, giving you just one minute per idea.

Step 2: The rules

There's just one rule: fill each section with a different idea within the one-minute time limit. It's all about quick thinking, not perfect execution. Sketch, scribble, or jot down keywords – whatever helps you express your idea.

Take a second and go grab a pencil and a sheet of paper; we're about to get creative! Set up your Crazy 8 framework and come up with some solutions for our cash-strapped founder's problem. Remember not to overthink it – this is supposed to be a quick and fun exercise to get those creative juices flowing.

Let's dive into some of the ideas that I generated from completing this framework:

1. **Freelance platforms:** An expert-for-hire platform that helps startups hire the expertise they need when they need it.

2. **Virtual assistants:** Use AI-based virtual assistants for administrative tasks. They can manage calendars, send reminders, and even handle customer service inquiries, helping founders save time and money.

3. **Automated workflows:** A tool that helps startups create automations of the most time-consuming tasks.

4. **Internship programs:** A platform that connects students and graduates with startups for a range of internship opportunities.

5. **Crowdsourcing platforms:** A crowdsourcing platform to buy much-needed assets that every startup needs, such as graphics, content, and Excel templates.

6. **Easy hire:** A platform that helps startups find and hire the right people at the right time, saving money and resources.

7. **Sales platform:** A sales tool that helps businesses improve their revenue streams, in turn allowing them the required growth capital to hire team members.

8. **Crowdfunding app:** A tool that helps startups find investors who would provide the required capital to hire team members in return for an equity stake.

As you can see, the Crazy 8s framework has helped us generate a broad range of solutions, each tackling the problem from a unique angle. Some ideas might seem more feasible or practical than others, but that's the beauty of this exercise. It's about letting your creative juices flow freely, challenging assumptions, and seeing the problem from fresh perspectives.

The beauty of the Crazy 8s framework is in its speed and efficiency. It bypasses our natural inclination to overthink and self-censor, pushing us to spill out ideas without judgment or inhibition. This process can bring forward some surprising solutions that you might not have considered in a more conventional brainstorming session.

Remember, this is just the beginning. Once you have your ideas on paper, you can start refining them, merging similar ones, discarding the impractical ones, and expanding on the promising ones. With each iteration, your solution will become more concrete and tailored to your problem.

The most important takeaway from this exercise is not the ideas themselves but the process of generating them. It's about embracing the creative chaos, breaking free from linear thinking, and realizing that there's not just one but multiple ways to solve a problem. The Crazy 8s framework is a powerful tool in your ideation arsenal. Use it whenever you're stuck or need to look at a problem from a different angle.

The journey from identifying a problem to finding a solution is a thrilling adventure. It's filled with challenges, twists, and turns, but each step brings you closer to your entrepreneurial goal. With the Crazy 8s framework, you're equipped with a technique that can propel your ideas forward, providing a springboard for your creativity. So, take out that paper, start folding, and let the ideas flow – your solution is waiting to be discovered.

Researching your potential market

In the landscape of entrepreneurship, the task of creating a solution for a problem is just the first leg of the journey. Once a solution is conceptualized, the next, equally important step is to research the idea in the marketplace. This research is crucial as it determines the viability of your idea in the real world and helps identify the possible competitors in the market.

When I set about creating Willo.Social, a platform designed to help individuals with chronic health conditions find local friends for symptom-appropriate sports and social activities, I had first-hand experience of the problem at hand. I knew what I wanted to offer my customers. However, before proceeding, it was vital to investigate the landscape and see what solutions were already available in the market.

What solutions are there already, and how are they not working?

To begin with, I turned to my customers themselves. In the course of discussing their problems, they mentioned various platforms they were already using to find companionship and activities. These included Meetup.com, Eventbrite, Facebook Groups, and a couple of niche apps for specific conditions. I listed these in a spreadsheet and started a deep dive into each one. I looked at their offerings, pricing structures, strengths, and weaknesses. Each piece of data was meticulously noted.

Next, I took my research to the wider internet. I searched through app marketplaces, industry magazines, and blogs, looking for potential competitors. I also paid particular attention to customer reviews and feedback. These are often goldmines of information, as customers frequently post about what they can't do with a service or what they wish it would offer. Such insights can guide you towards unmet needs in the market and areas you can capitalize on.

I created a feature list comparing what my competitors offered their customers. This was an excellent way to identify gaps in the market and potential unique selling points (USPs) for Willo.Social.

How much money is there in this area?

Investor trends are another crucial part of market research. Where are investors putting their money in your sector? If venture capitalists are investing, it's a good indicator that customers are spending money in that area.

What is the scale and the opportunity of my market?

Government statistical sites can also provide invaluable data. These can help you understand the scale of the problem you're tackling, its cost to the economy, and the potential opportunities within it. Also, take a look at consumer trend reports, many of which you will find online through doing a quick Google search.

How to conduct user research

When conducting such extensive research, the organization is key. Tools like Excel or Google Sheets are great for keeping data structured and accessible. For qualitative data, a tool like Notion can help keep your notes and observations organized.

In today's age, artificial intelligence (AI) can also be a valuable ally in market research. An AI tool like ChatGPT, developed by OpenAI, can help analyze large volumes of data, identify trends, and even generate insights. Its natural language processing ability can be used to sift through customer reviews and feedback across multiple platforms and extract useful information.

Researching your idea in the marketplace is a vital step in the entrepreneurial journey. It helps you understand your competition, identify gaps in the market, and fine-tune your solution to better meet the needs of your customers. While it can be a time-consuming process, the insights gained can be the difference between the success and failure of your startup. Remember, there's no such thing as too much information when it comes to understanding your market.

How to find and interview potential customers

Comprehending your potential customers is a fundamental element of successful entrepreneurship. This understanding is rooted in thorough customer profiling and careful interviewing, which helps ensure your product or service matches market needs, engages users, and fosters the growth of your business. These practices are applicable irrespective of whether your target audience is B2C (Business to Commerce) or B2B (Business to Business).

Identifying potential customers for interviews in the B2C sector necessitates an understanding of their online and offline gathering spots. These could range from various social media platforms to online forums, local community groups, or offline events. For B2B, tapping into professional networks like LinkedIn, industry-specific forums, trade shows, and business conferences are strategic avenues.

When initiating contact with potential interviewees, it's crucial to maintain transparency and a courteous tone. Clearly explain who you are and why you're conducting this research, and reassure them of the importance and value of their contributions. If you intend to record the conversation, seek their consent in advance to respect their rights and also to ensure you have an accurate reference for their feedback.

Keep a systematic method to document responses during interviews. An unbiased, meticulous record not only facilitates a seamless reference to the feedback later but also enables effective analysis. Using a spreadsheet to categorize this information can prove to be quite effective.

A crucial aspect of this process is defining and refining your customer base. It can sometimes be a challenge, as I found during my initial startup endeavour. We were developing a product aimed at individuals wishing to better manage their mental health. Initially, our approach was broad; we interviewed anyone with any experience of mental health issues. However, we soon realized that although they shared some general issues, the nuances of their experiences resulted in hundreds of unique problems. This taught us the importance of targeted focus on a specific customer base. Our ultimate customers were HR Directors seeking to provide supportive tools to their staff to handle anxiety and stress. This realization could have come earlier had we crafted precise personas from the start.

The application of this methodology proved crucial during the development of Willo.Social, allowing us to identify three primary challenges our potential customers faced: a lack of appropriate local support groups, difficulty participating in desired activities due to their unique needs, and uncertainty about what activities would be most suitable given their symptoms. This understanding shaped the development and offerings of Willo.Social.

Crafting the perfect interview request email

There will likely come a point where you exhaust your immediate network when it comes to arranging interviews. Instead, you're going to have to either pick up the phone and do some cold outreach, and/or you're going to have to connect with users via a polite email. This is a template that I use to connect with users via Linkedin or private company emails:

Subject: Invitation for a Brief Discussion About [Problem Sector]

Dear [First Name],

My name is [Your Name], and I'm a product developer exploring a solution in the [problem sector]. As a [relevant characteristic/job/role], your insights would be incredibly valuable to our research.

Would you be open to a confidential, 30-minute call to discuss the challenges you face concerning [specific task/ role]? Your input could help shape a solution that meets user needs in this domain.

I look forward to your response.

Best,

[Your Name]

In the following section, we will delve into the creation of this email capture page and discuss how it serves as an initial step in the journey of transforming interested individuals into potential customers.

Build an automated email capture

An important step for me is creating an email capture. This is a simple one-page website that contains some basic information about your business and a form that asks users to submit their name and email. It may be that they want to receive product updates or they would like to schedule an interview. If lots of people are signing up for updates then it's a good indication that there is some interest in what you're doing.

If you haven't built an email capture page before, don't worry! I'm about to take you through the simple steps you need to get it up online and collecting email data.

The first step in this process is to create a landing page where you'll host your form. You can accomplish this with website builders like WordPress, Wix, or Webflow. These platforms make it easy to design and launch a webpage without needing to delve into coding.

However, if your focus is sharing the form through social media posts or emails, you might prefer using a stand-alone form generator. Tools such as Mailchimp, JotForm, or Google Forms are excellent for this purpose. Ideally, your form should collect the user's name, email, and job title (especially important for B2B products). These tools also offer an 'embed' feature, enabling you to integrate the form into an email or webpage, providing a seamless experience for your users.

An integral part of this process is securely storing the collected emails. Services like Mailchimp offer storage facilities, starting with a free tier and moving into subscription-based plans as your database grows. Alternatively, you could consider using a spreadsheet, but beware of potential security risks. Regardless of your chosen method, remember to comply with your country's privacy laws and data protection regulations.

In the case of Willo.Social, we used WordPress to set up a simple landing page. After purchasing a domain name and hosting service, we used Mailchimp to create an embedded form for email capture. The user-friendly interface of Mailchimp also allowed us to integrate with

Calendly, a meeting scheduling tool, setting up 30-minute slots for Zoom calls.

The integration between Mailchimp and Calendly meant that every time a user scheduled an interview, I received a notification, and the user received a confirmation email with the Zoom link. This automated system streamlined the process, saving time, and reducing the scope for error.

For instances where your chosen tools do not offer direct integrations, automation platforms like Zapier or Integromat can bridge the gap. They can connect your calendar to your email capture system, making your workflow more efficient. We'll delve deeper into these automation tools later.

Now that you have an overview, it's time for you to experiment. Create an email capture form and meeting scheduler tailored to your idea. This hands-on experience will deepen your understanding of the tools and processes, equipping you for the challenges of your startup journey. My suggestion is that you start with creating a form first because you can then easily embed this straight into your social pages and emails. You can do the old-fashioned 'what time are you free?' questions back and forth with the interviewee, but creating a meeting scheduler will save you and your new potential customers time and hassle. Creating a streamlined and quick service is more likely to win you a meeting than by putting lots of communication roadblocks in the way.

3

Planning your MVP

What is an MVP?

You may have heard of something called a 'Minimum Viable Product'. This is a foundational step in the development of your business, as your MVP will serve as the first tangible representation of your idea that you can put into the hands of your customers.

An MVP is the most simplified version of your product that still delivers its core value proposition. It's designed to provide immediate value quickly while minimizing development costs. The MVP is not about creating a cheaper product; it's about learning. It allows you to validate your assumptions, gain user insights, test the market, and iterate based on feedback. Simply put, an MVP is the smallest thing you can build that delivers customer value and, in a return, allows you to learn from it.

One entrepreneur's story serves as a stark reminder of why starting with an MVP is crucial. This individual conceived a new mobile dating app. She decided to skip the customer discovery phase and went straight to app development, spending close to £70,000 to get the app professionally built. The app had every feature she could imagine, most of them unvalidated with her target audience.

When she launched the app, it flopped. Some of her assumptions about her user base were correct, but the solution she built didn't meet their needs effectively. The extravagant features she thought were necessary proved to be irrelevant to her users. Had she started with an MVP, she could have saved a significant amount of money and time, refined her idea based on real-world feedback, and, most importantly, reduced the risk of failure.

Contrast this story with the beginnings of companies like Airbnb and Amazon. Airbnb's MVP was a simple website offering short-term living quarters and breakfast for those who were unable to book a hotel in the saturated San Francisco market. The idea was not to create the largest global marketplace for lodgings but to solve an immediate problem. They wanted to validate if people were comfortable staying in strangers' homes and they did that without building anything too extravagant.

Similarly, when Amazon first started, it was not the massive online marketplace it is today. Amazon's MVP was a simple online platform selling books. Jeff Bezos, the founder of Amazon, chose books because they were low-cost and universally demanded. By selling books online, Amazon was testing the broader assumption of whether customers were ready to buy products online. The success of this MVP validated the idea, and Amazon gradually expanded into selling virtually everything.

These examples emphasize the power and importance of an MVP. It allows you to validate your ideas, save time and money, and decrease risk. An MVP focuses on the main problem your business is solving and uses the simplest method to address it. By launching an MVP, you can learn from your customers' feedback, iteratively improve your product, and build something that truly meets their needs. The focus should always be on learning and adapting, not on delivering a perfect product in the first instance. In the next sections, we'll delve deeper into how to build an MVP using no-code tools, helping you to get your product into the market quickly and economically.

Testing our business assumptions

The journey from customer discovery to the creation of an MVP is a vital one in the entrepreneurial process. At this stage, we take the research we've gathered, distilled it down to the most prominent problems our customer is facing, and we've begun to ideate potential solutions.

With Willo.Social, I became super focused on the three biggest problems that my potential customers were experiencing. We discussed earlier how we can use the Crazy 8 framework to generate ideas. That's exactly what I did here, taking each of the problems one by one and completing the framework. The nature of the ideas spanned a broad spectrum – from digital community management for peer-driven support groups, to an events-style board for symptom-based meetups. After repeating this process for all three problems, the skeleton of a product began to emerge – a product that could potentially offer solutions to these three significant issues. This was the early inception of Willo.Social.

Let's revisit our earlier example of a startup that lacks the resources to hire a full-time team member. To make life easier, let's call our new imaginary startup 'StartRight'. One of the solutions we brainstormed was a platform that connected startups with freelance experts. Through our customer conversations, we discovered that startups often require short-term expertise to help them navigate a series of challenges as they grow their organization within the first three years. Unfortunately, they don't always know who to ask or how to find these experts, a big problem for first-time founders with a limited network.

When we're formulating product ideas, our focus should be on resolving the core problem our customer faces, which in this case, is the need to solve problems that allows their business to flourish. Our initial idea is to create a marketplace platform that facilitates connections between startups and experts, offering a pay-as-you-go solution to cash-strapped businesses. The platform would handle the administrative aspects, including payment.

Now comes a critical phase – testing what we think our customers want. We're making three key assumptions here:

1. Startups will hire experts on a pay-as-they-need basis.

2. Experts will sell their time to startups.

3. Experts will sell their time through our platform, paying a commission on every sale.

If any of these assumptions prove false, the entire business proposition is at risk. This is why our next step is to validate these assumptions in the most economical and efficient way possible.

Our process to test these assumptions would be:

1. **Define the assumptions:** Articulate your hypotheses clearly. In our case, we believe that startups and freelance experts will find value in our proposition.

2. **Design the tests:** Outline how you will validate each assumption. We might reach out to startups and experts to gauge interest or make connections with startup accelerators and business hubs. We could also use our data-collecting tool to ask people to sign up to a waiting list. If we see that there are a large number of startups and experts waiting to use what we build then we know we have at least struck a chord.

3. **Execute the tests:** Carry out your tests, whether they are surveys, interviews, or exploratory meetings. This step is about gathering data. One of my favourite ways to validate my idea is to create wireframes of my product idea. We'll go deeper into what wireframes are later, but essentially, they're a graphic-based representation of what our app will look like. You can show these to your potential customers to get quick feedback.

4. **Evaluate the results:** Interpret the data you've collected. Do the results confirm or refute your hypotheses? If they align, you've got the go-ahead. If not, it's back to the drawing board.

5. **Iterate:** This process is cyclical – you'll continually make assumptions, test them, evaluate the results, and revise your product idea as needed.

Ultimately, the goal is to identify the key assumptions underlying your product idea and to test these assumptions in the most efficient and cost-effective way possible. In doing so, you minimize risk and increase the likelihood that your final product will resonate with your intended audience. Of course, building our MVP in no-code tools is a really great way to execute your tests, but it's even better when you've already got some of your assumptions partly answered.

Examples of MVPs

When we think of an MVP, we will more often than not, think of a piece of functioning software that automates a series of helpful steps for our customer. Certainly, years ago, I'd get so hung up on the ideas that I'd need a developer to code something impressive so that I could prove that my idea had legs. However, once I dug a little deeper, I learned that MVPs actually comes in many different forms. Let's take a look at some of the most popular to see if you could apply these methods to your own idea.

Wizard of Oz MVP

In this approach, the product's functions are manually carried out by the team behind the scenes, but sometimes give the impression of a sophisticated product. It's a way to validate the need for a solution without building the actual automated system. A great example of the Wizard of Oz MVP is by a company called Zappos.

Problem identification: Nick Swinmurn, the founder of Zappos, identified a problem: people might want to buy shoes online, but there was uncertainty about whether consumers would be comfortable buying shoes without trying them on first.

Testing the hypothesis: Instead of building a full-fledged e-commerce platform with inventory, Swinmurn decided to test the basic hypothesis. He went to local shoe stores, took pictures of the shoes, and posted them online.

Manual fulfillment: When someone ordered a pair of shoes from his website, Swinmurn would go back to the store, buy the shoes, and then ship them to the customer. This process was entirely manual, and the store owners didn't even know he was doing this.

Validation: The Concierge MVP allowed Swinmurn to validate that there was demand for buying shoes online. The manual process helped him understand customer preferences, pain points, and the logistics involved without a significant upfront investment.

Scaling: Once the concept was validated, Zappos built its own inventory and logistics system, eventually becoming one of the largest online shoe retailers. The company was later acquired by Amazon for $1.2 billion in 2009.

Concierge MVP

A concierge MVP is very similar to a Wizard of Oz MVP, except that technology is usually not involved. A great example of this was a company called Food on The Table.

Concept: Food on the Table aimed to help families plan meals based on their food preferences and the sales at local grocery stores. The idea was to provide weekly meal plans and shopping lists tailored to what's on sale, ensuring users get variety in their meals while also saving money.

Testing the hypothesis: Instead of building an app or a platform right away, the founder, Manuel Rosso, started by personally assisting a few families. He went to their homes, interviewed them about their food preferences, checked local grocery store sales manually, and then provided them with a weekly meal plan and shopping list.

Manual service: Rosso personally delivered the meal plans and shopping lists to these families every week. He also took feedback on the meals, what worked, what didn't, and any other preferences or constraints the families had.

Validation: This hands-on approach allowed Rosso to deeply understand the pain points and needs of his target audience. He could refine the service based on direct feedback and understand the intricacies of meal planning in conjunction with grocery store sales.

Scaling: After validating the concept and understanding the user needs, Food on the Table developed a mobile app and web platform that automated the process. Users could input their preferences, and the platform would generate meal plans and shopping lists based on local sales.

Growth and acquisition: The startup grew rapidly, reaching hundreds of thousands of users. In 2013, Food on the Table was acquired by the Scripps Network.

Single feature MVP

Instead of building a product with multiple features, the team focuses on creating a single feature that addresses the core problem. This helps in understanding the value and demand for that particular feature. Uber is a great example of a startup that utilized the single-feature MVP approach.

Origins: Uber began as 'UberCab' in 2009, founded by Garrett Camp and Travis Kalanick. The initial idea was born out of personal frustration with the difficulty of hailing a taxi in San Francisco.

Single feature: The primary feature of UberCab was simple: allow users to request a luxury car ride using just their smartphone. There were no multiple-ride options like UberX, UberPOOL, or UberEATS. It was just a black car service requested via an app.

Testing the hypothesis: The founders started by offering rides in San Francisco using only three cars to test the concept and gauge interest. Users could request a ride using the app, and a high-end vehicle (like a Mercedes) would pick them up.

Validation: The immediate positive response from early users in San Francisco indicated that there was a demand for such a service. People loved the convenience, the predictability of the wait time, and the experience of riding in a luxury vehicle.

Pricing model: The initial pricing was straightforward, with a base fare plus additional charges based on time and distance. Surge pricing and other pricing models came later as the platform evolved.

Evolution and growth: As the concept was validated and demand grew, Uber began expanding to other cities and introduced additional features and services. They launched UberX (a less expensive option using everyday cars), followed by various other services like UberPOOL (ridesharing) and UberEATS (food delivery). But at its inception, the MVP was solely about requesting a luxury car ride via an app.

Landing page MVP

Before developing the product, a landing page is set up to describe the product's value proposition and features. Interested users can sign up or pre-order. This helps in gauging interest and demand. A classic example of a startup that effectively utilized a landing page MVP is Dropbox.

Concept: Dropbox aimed to provide a simple and efficient solution for file synchronization and sharing across devices. While the idea sounds commonplace now, at the time, it was a novel solution to a widespread problem.

Testing the hypothesis: Instead of waiting to perfect the product or trying to explain the concept with just text, Drew Houston, the founder, created a simple explainer video that demonstrated how Dropbox would work. This video was the centrepiece of their landing page.

Landing page elements: The Dropbox landing page had:

- The explainer video.

- A brief description of the product.

- An invitation for users to sign up for early access.

Validation: The video went viral in tech communities. Overnight, the waiting list for Dropbox went from 5,000 people to over 75,000. This massive surge in interest validated a significant demand for the solution Dropbox was proposing.

Feedback and iteration: The landing page not only gauged interest but also provided an avenue for potential users to give feedback, helping the Dropbox team refine their product before the public launch.

Product launch and growth: Armed with validation and user feedback, Dropbox launched its product, which quickly gained traction. Today, it's one of the leading file synchronization and cloud storage services globally.

Choosing the right type of MVP

Selecting the right MVP hinges on various factors, including time constraints and budget, which are unique to your situation. I've experienced moments where I developed one kind of MVP, only to pivot to another when I realized it would provide clearer insights. The key is to pinpoint the assumptions you're aiming to validate. Ask yourself: What's the most efficient way to address these assumptions? If you're solely gauging market interest, a landing page MVP could be ideal. However, if you're assessing a user's willingness to purchase, a Wizard of Oz or a single-feature product might be more fitting. Fortunately, with no-code platforms, crafting any of these MVPs becomes incredibly straightforward!

Using the MoSCoW framework to revise your MVP

When embarking on a new product development journey, it's all too easy to get swept away in the tide of creative ideas. From elaborate features to intricate designs, these concepts can quickly pile up, muddling your clarity and overwhelming your development process. This is where the MoSCoW framework steps in, providing a robust method to prioritize features and maintain focus on the essence of your product.

The MoSCoW framework is an agile prioritization technique which stands for Must-have, Should-have, Could-have, and Won't-have (or not just yet). By placing your proposed features into these categories, you can streamline your approach, ensure that the most crucial elements are addressed, and avoid getting distracted by less critical extras. I use this framework a lot because I'm one of those people whose ideas race ahead of me.

During my mental health startup, we used the MoSCoW method to drill down into the features we needed for our mobile app. As a complex piece of software, it was vital that we spent our time on the necessary features. The MoSCoW framework provided a systematic method to boil down the core components we absolutely needed. At the time, it really helped that we had a development team who could help us bounce ideas around. It's not absolutely necessary, but I would recommend getting a couple of friends around to help you with this activity. Sometimes, it's easier for someone on the outside to say, 'You really don't need that'. Later, in the development of Willo.Social, the framework proved invaluable in discerning the essential features from the nice-to-haves. I imagine if I'd gone with everything I'd wanted, I'd probably still be building rather than getting it out into the hands of customers.

Let's examine how this framework can be applied to 'StartRight', our amazing imaginary startup.

On a whiteboard or a large piece of paper, divided into four sections labelled M (Must-have), S (Should-have), C (Could-have), and W (Won't-have (yet)). Grab a stack of sticky notes, each bearing a potential feature for your app. The task at hand is to allocate each sticky note to one of the four sections on your board.

In the Must-have category, we have the features that are essential for the basic functionality of our app. Without these, the app simply cannot operate. For our marketplace app, these would be:

1. **User registration and login system:** Both startups and experts need to have personal accounts to use the service.

2. **Search feature to find experts by skill:** Startups need to locate experts according to their needs.

3. **Service creation:** Our experts need to create a service that they will be selling to our startups.

4. **Payment system:** A full end-to-end order management and payment system between our startup and our experts.

5. **In-house chat feature:** Allows our startups and expert to communicate with each other without leaving the app.

Next, we have the Should-have category. These are features that are important but not critical to the app's primary function. Our app would function without them, but they significantly enhance its value. For our app, these might include:

1. **Expert reviews:** The ability for startups to leave a 1–5 star review and comment about the expert that they hired.

2. **Expert and 'Startup of the Month' feature:** This could select and highlight work that had been completed over the last month.

3. **Monthly newsletters:** This could improve engagement with our startup customers.

The Could-have category includes features that are nice to have but are not necessary for the app to perform its primary function. They could be postponed without a significant impact on the customer experience. For our startup-expert app, these might be:

1. **Video profiles:** Experts leave a video message promoting their service or skill.

2. **A forum:** For experts to post ideas and advice for each other.

Lastly, the Won't-have category includes features that we decide not to include in this development cycle. These might be irrelevant to the app's core function, too costly to develop, or better suited for future versions. Our startup app might leave out the following:

1. **Course creation:** Experts can sell short courses as a secondary income.

2. **Monthly video workshops:** For our startups led by one of our experts.

By going through this process, you can gain clarity on your product vision, focus your resources where they matter most, and ensure you're delivering value to your customers.

From MoSCoW to flowchart

After I've completed the MoSCoW framework and I have my list of essential features, I like to grab some sheets of paper and jot some ideas down. I start with a simple flow chart of my user journey. This helps me to map out how I want my customer to use my app, what pages I will require and what features I need on each screen This doesn't have to be perfect or technical. This is just a rough guide to help you get to the next step. Figure 3.1 is an example of a flowchart I created for Willo.Social in the very early days.

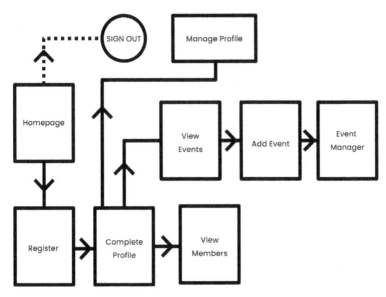

Figure 3.1 Flowchart

From doing this, I was able to plan out that my user begins at a landing page and then went through a registration and onboarding process. I like to break my onboarding screens down into several linked pages, so that the user isn't presented with a long form which they need to scroll through. So, on page one I ask for their name, email, and password; on page two I ask them about their business and location; on page 3 I ask for a profile pic and their location.

In terms of users of my app I can see that we have two distinct customer types: the startup and the expert.

First, let's look at the ideal journey of a startup user. The founder or representative of the company will arrive at the landing page, which will offer a quick search function for experts. We want our startups to see what type of experts are on our site and who they could be working with. They'll be able to use search terms like 'advertising', 'investment', or 'sales'.

They will be taken to a product page detailing the experts working within that field. It will show a short bio, including their price. Clicking on an expert takes them to their full bio.

If they decide to buy the service the expert is offering, they move to a payment page and, finally, the 'contact the expert' page, where they can communicate with each other about the next steps.

If we look at the expert's journey, they, too, will arrive at the landing page before moving on to a registration page where they can enter their details. They will then be taken to a profile page where they can move through creating their full bio.

On the 'add service' page, they can set up their service offering, including cost. From here they will be linked straight into their dashboard, where they can see any orders that have taken place and how much money they have generated that month. Figure 3.2 outlines this principle in the form of an expert flowchart.

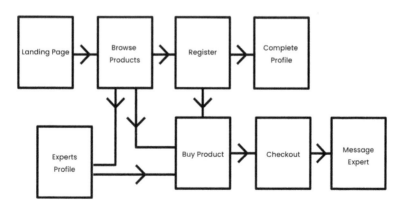

Figure 3.2 Experts flowchart

Activity: Create your first flowchart

Take your must-have feature list and create a simple flow chart for your own user journey. You can use pen and paper, or there are several whiteboard tools online, such as Miro or Canva.

4

Creating and testing visual prototypes

Ever faced the daunting challenge of sketching a self-portrait on a pristine sheet of paper? That initial hesitation, the uncertainty of where to begin, the multiple attempts to get the eyes just right or the nose in proportion – it's a feeling many can relate to. Skilled artists often start with a basic outline, mapping out facial features and the overall composition. Only when satisfied do they proceed with the final drawing. Similarly, if I were to ask you to design an app from scratch, you might be overwhelmed by the digital equivalent of that 'blank page'. Diving in without a plan might result in a design that's not only aesthetically off but also confusing for users. This is where visual prototyping comes into play. Let's delve into two primary forms of prototyping: low fidelity and high fidelity, exploring their purposes and when to employ each.

What are low-fidelity prototypes?

Low-fidelity (lo-fi) prototypes are simplistic, often non-interactive models of your product. Essentially, they're the rough sketches of your product idea that serve to illustrate its basic structure and functionality. Lo-fi prototypes could take the form of hand-drawn illustrations, wireframes, or even a storyboard.

These prototypes lack the visual refinement and detailed features that high-fidelity prototypes have. But they provide a clear enough representation of the product's fundamental design and layout, enabling the validation of essential user flows and features at an early stage.

When should you use low-fidelity prototypes?

You should use low-fidelity prototypes during the initial stages of your product development process. Since they are quick and inexpensive to create, they're perfect for validating the core concept of your product.

Low-fidelity prototypes encourage broad feedback because the simplicity of the design allows users, stakeholders, and team members to focus on the functionality and user experience rather than the visual and aesthetic aspects of the product.

Lo-fi prototypes are instrumental in spotting usability issues and gathering initial user feedback. They provide an excellent platform for brainstorming, user testing, and iterative design without committing excessive resources to an unvalidated idea. They allow your team to fail fast, learn quickly, and adapt the design before moving on to the more detailed stages of development. In essence, low-fidelity prototyping ensures that you are building the 'right it' before you start building 'it right'.

What are high-fidelity prototypes?

High-fidelity (hi-fi) prototypes are detailed, often interactive, representations of your product. These prototypes include the precise layout, design elements, interactions, and often the content, making them appear and function as close to the final product as possible.

These prototypes allow for a realistic user experience simulation, enabling users, stakeholders, and developers to see and interact with a near-final product version. They give a clear visual and practical understanding of how the product will look and feel in the real world.

When should you use high-fidelity prototypes?

High-fidelity prototypes should be employed later in the design process once the product's core concept, structure, and user flows have been validated with a low-fidelity prototype.

Since these prototypes closely mimic the final product's look and functionality, they are crucial for conducting detailed usability testing. Hi-fi prototypes can help detect any remaining usability issues, verify the effectiveness of the UI (user interface) design, and assess the overall user experience. They also serve as an excellent demonstration model for stakeholders, clients, or potential investors.

High-fidelity prototypes are time-consuming and require more resources to create. Therefore, they should be used when you need to ensure that you're not just building the 'right it', but you're also building 'it right'. Don't worry if you're not a designer. Many no-code platforms offer design tools which we'll discuss in depth later.

Types of low-fidelity tools

The beauty of low-fidelity prototyping is that you don't need any fancy equipment or software to get started. In fact, one of the most effective tools for low-fidelity prototyping is a simple pencil.

Yes, you heard that right. A pencil offers a cheap, highly portable, and versatile means to sketch out your ideas quickly. You can erase and modify your design easily, allowing for immediate iteration based on your thoughts or feedback.

Pair a pencil with a sheet of paper, and you've got a portable design studio at your fingertips!

To aid your sketching process, there are numerous free templates available online for both web and mobile design. If you're looking for a ready-made set of templates, our website, https://nocodestartup.co/templates, offers a variety of printable resources that you can use.

What you're aiming to create at this stage is a 'wireframe'. A wireframe is a basic visual guide that represents the skeletal framework of your product. It's like the blueprint of a building; it shows where elements will be placed without focusing on aesthetics. By sketching wireframes of your product, you can map out the structure, layout, and functionality effectively.

Moving into the digital realm, there's a broad spectrum of online tools available for creating low-fidelity prototypes. One of the standout tools is Figma, an offering from Adobe. Figma caters to both beginners and seasoned designers alike with its user-friendly interface and rich feature set. Not only can you create straightforward wireframes, but you can also link screens together, make elements interactive, and even demonstrate basic animations. This functionality allows for a higher level of user testing, giving users a realistic experience of navigating your prototype.

Miro is another impressive tool for creating low-fidelity prototypes. Miro functions as an expansive online whiteboard where you can design wireframes, collate design ideas, and make notes. Its vast array of templates and intuitive drag-and-drop interface streamlines the prototyping process, helping you flesh out your ideas with ease.

One of the unique selling points of Miro is its integration capabilities. You can connect it with other tools like Zoom, Slack, and Google Drive, enabling a seamless workflow. This integration allows you to keep all your notes, flow diagrams, and other resources in one accessible location, promoting a cohesive design process.

Whether you opt for traditional pencil and paper or digital platforms like Figma and Miro, the key focus in low-fidelity prototyping is to quickly and cheaply visualize your ideas. These tools allow you to rapidly test and iterate your concepts, paving the way towards a well-structured, user-focused product.

Activity: Creating your first low-fidelity prototype

Jumping straight into the build phase without a concrete plan can lead to missteps and costly changes later. That's why it's essential to start with a low-fidelity prototype, a rudimentary visual representation of your product's layout and flow. Go ahead and try creating your first low-fidelity prototype using just a pencil and paper.

Step 1: Identify the key components

Begin by brainstorming the key components of your application. These might include login screens, dashboards, navigation menus, content areas, and interactive elements like buttons or forms. Take into account whether your application will be mobile or desktop-based, as this will affect the layout and design.

For a mobile application, consider the limited screen real estate and how users will interact using touch. On the other hand, a desktop application might afford more space and complex interactions but needs to be intuitive for users navigating with a mouse or trackpad.

Step 2: Sketch the basic layout

Now that you've identified the components, it's time to bring out your pencil and paper. Start drawing basic shapes to represent these elements. A rectangle might symbolize a content area, circles could denote buttons, and lines might indicate text or dividing sections.

Remember, at this stage, your focus is not on aesthetics but on functionality and user experience. Your sketch should illustrate how a user would navigate your app, how the elements are organized, and how information is presented.

Step 3: Iterating Your sketches

Once you've sketched the basic layout, take a step back and review your work. Does the flow make sense? Is it easy for a user to navigate from one section to another? Is the critical content readily accessible?

Don't be afraid to make changes at this stage. In fact, one of the major benefits of using pencil and paper is the ease with which you can erase and modify your design. Iteration is an integral part of the design process, and it's much easier and cheaper to make changes now than during the development phase.

Step 4: Simulate the user journey

Once you're satisfied with the layout and flow, try to simulate a user's journey. Imagine you're a first-time user of your app. Start from the home or login screen and navigate through the various sections and features. This exercise can provide valuable insights into your design's strengths and potential areas of improvement.

Gathering feedback: The crucial step in refining your prototype

It is often said that the customer is always right. When it comes to designing a prototype for a new product or service, it's no different. Gathering feedback from your customers or potential users is a crucial step in the prototyping process. It allows you to begin testing those early assumptions, identify usability issues, and understand whether or not the prototype aligns with the needs of your target audience.

How to gather feedback on visual prototypes

In the first days of your startup you will have been out meeting and talking to potential customers and posing the right questions to discover their painful points. Now that you have a visual prototype, how do you gather their genuine feelings about your product? Well, there are several ways to gather this feedback.

1. **In-person testing:** Organize a session where your potential users can interact with your prototype. Observe them closely, see how they interact with it, where they face challenges, and what they intuitively understand. Take notes or, if possible, record these sessions (with their consent, of course) for future reference. What might be even more helpful is if you can stay out of the room entirely. Get someone who is not connected with the business to sit with the user and gather their raw feedback. If you're there and they know you're the founder, they might feel like they can't be 100% honest.

2. **Virtual testing:** In situations where in-person meetings are not feasible, virtual testing is an excellent alternative. There are numerous tools available that allow users to interact with your prototype remotely while you observe their interactions (either live or through heatmap recordings). A tool like Hotjar tracks your users mouse movements so that you can see how they're using your product. You can even use share-screen on tools such as Zoom (just remember to ask permission if you wish to record the session).

3. **Surveys and questionnaires:** While they don't provide as detailed insights as live observations, surveys

and questionnaires can be a good way to gather quantitative feedback.

Understanding the feedback

Once you have gathered feedback, it's time to make sense of it. Look for patterns – are many users facing the same issues or expressing similar concerns?

Not all feedback will be relevant, and you may encounter individuals who simply do not resonate with your prototype. That's okay. As you gather more feedback, you'll begin to understand what's an isolated opinion and what's a common trend.

When to pivot: Making sense of mixed feedback

A common challenge while gathering feedback is receiving mixed signals. Some users may love your prototype, while others might not find it appealing or useful. So, when do you decide to pivot or stick to your guns?

As a general rule of thumb, if over 70% of your audience is satisfied with your prototype, you're on the right track. However, if you find that half or more of your audience needs clarification, it's time to go back to the drawing board and iterate.

Iterating and pivoting: Refining based on feedback

The process of refining your prototype based on feedback involves iterating your design, making changes and tweaks, and then testing it again. This is not a one-time process but a cycle that continues until you achieve a design that most of your users are happy with.

In conclusion, gathering feedback on your prototype is a critical process that helps validate your ideas and refine your design based on real-world insights. Remember, your goal is to

create a product that serves your users effectively, and their feedback is the most potent tool in achieving this. It's an ongoing, iterative process that requires resilience and adaptability.

Acting on feedback: Listening vs. implementing

Understanding feedback is one thing; knowing what to do with it is another. It's essential to remember that feedback comes in many forms and from many sources. It's critical to understand that not all feedback is created equal, and acting on every piece of feedback you receive is not always necessary.

When assessing feedback, it's crucial to identify whether the feedback is a usability issue (something that hinders the user experience) or a feature request (something that a user would 'like' to see). Usability issues should be addressed as quickly as possible, while feature requests should be evaluated based on your product vision, resources, and overall product roadmap.

Contextualizing feedback: The big picture

Context matters when it comes to feedback. It's vital to consider the context in which the feedback was given. Was it a casual comment, or did it come from a structured testing session? How familiar is the person with the type of product you're creating? Are they a potential user or is someone giving an outside opinion?

Each piece of feedback needs to be considered in light of these questions. This will help you gauge the importance and relevance of the feedback and understand how much weight it should carry in your decision-making process.

Consolidating feedback: Identifying patterns

After gathering feedback, it's time to consolidate the information. Look for commonalities or patterns in the feedback. If multiple users are expressing similar issues or suggestions, it's an indication that these areas need your attention.

It's also helpful to categorize feedback into different buckets. This could be 'usability issues', 'feature requests', 'design feedback', etc. This process of categorization can help you make sense of the feedback and decide on your next steps.

From feedback to action: The iterative process

The process of transforming feedback into actionable improvements involves an iterative cycle of refining, testing, and learning. Each cycle brings you closer to a product that better aligns with your user's needs and expectations.

It's important to approach this process with an open mind. It's not about defending your initial design but about improving it based on user insights. Each round of feedback is a learning opportunity that brings you one step closer to creating a product that truly resonates with your audience.

In essence, gathering feedback on your prototype is not just about finding out what works or doesn't work; it's about learning, refining, and iterating until you have a product that serves your users effectively. While the process can be challenging and sometimes uncomfortable, the insights and improvements it leads to are invaluable. As you navigate the feedback process, remember to stay open, resilient, and focused on your ultimate goal: creating a product that your users love.

5

Building the back-end

What is the back-end of software development?

In simple terms, an app or website's back-end is the kitchen of a restaurant. We don't see it, but we know that's where all of our food is stored, where our orders are sent, and where our food is made before being sent out to us.

In the realm of software development, the 'back-end' (or server-side) signifies the unseen powerhouse behind any application or website that a user interacts with. It includes servers, databases, and applications that process any data that is sent from the user. While users don't interact with the back-end directly, it's responsible for storing, organizing, and processing data to ensure that the user-facing side (front-end) functions correctly. A back-end developer is someone who is responsible for creating and maintaining all of the features of a back-end, such as creating a database or writing code that tells a particular feature what to do when a user interacts with it.

A traditional back end is typically crafted using various programming languages like Java, Python, PHP, Ruby, .NET and coupled with database management systems such as MySQL, PostgreSQL, MongoDB, etc. The combination results in a robust infrastructure equipped to handle complex tasks and manage massive data loads.

For most individuals with an app idea (me included), the back-end has always been the part that made development nigh-on-impossible. Sure, it can be a little bit of a learning curve to pull together a well-designed app or website, but the true struggle always remained in getting the app to do wonderfully cool stuff. Throw in modern technologies like AI, and the accessibility of building apps was too far out of reach for the average non-coder. That is of course until no-code tools appeared on the market.

Back-end in no-code development

No-code development has reinvented the concept of back-end. The processes remain the same – all of the stuff that makes our app do stuff, but the method of execution has changed significantly. In no-code development, the back end is constructed using pre-made, customizable elements that are visually manipulated. It completely bypasses the need for writing any code, making the process more accessible.

The fundamental operations involved in back-end, such as data storage, retrieval, and management, are still the heart of the process. The change is in the tools used to accomplish these tasks. No-code development relies on user-friendly interfaces to implement and manipulate various aspects of back-end functionality, replacing lines of code with intuitive visual elements.

Choosing the right back-end tool

The type of back end in no-code development is closely tied to the application's nature and complexity. If you need to collect data (like user details or categories), then you will need to store that in a database.

For simple data collection or rudimentary applications, spreadsheet-style platforms like Google Sheets or Airtable often suffice. These platforms can act as a form of database, storing data inputted by users or by the app. The setup process is straightforward, with different columns representing various data points, and each row signifies a separate record. We then retrieve the data in our app with simple drag-and-drop commands. A great example of this is if we wanted to create a recipe app. We could create a simple spreadsheet that contained all our recipes. We could then display this list on our app for our user.

However, as well as a database, you may need to manipulate your data in some way, such as allowing users to search for recipes by keyword or category. No-code platforms such as Adalo, Bubble, and OutSystems not only offer internal database tools, but they also offer thousands of ready-built components that allow you to do some really interesting things with your data. One of my favourites is being to collect a user's event location and then display those details as a pin on a map.

Choosing the right database or 'back-end' system really depends on how complex your app is and what components you'll need. The choice also might be influenced by your preferred no-code platform. In my journey, I dedicated substantial time to practice building databases in Airtable to gain an in-depth understanding of how they worked. This hands-on experience proved invaluable in grasping the intricacies of database operation in a no-code context. As you venture on your journey, I encourage you to experiment, explore, and practice to find the tool that aligns best with your needs.

What is a relational database?

When setting out on any no-code journey, we inevitably encounter the concept of databases. They are the invisible engines that store, retrieve, and manage information in our applications. For a novice, databases can be quite perplexing. When I started, I remember feeling overwhelmed with all the technical jargon and myriad of options available. But over time, with a lot of practice and perseverance, particularly with accessible tools like Airtable, I found clarity. I started to appreciate the elegance and efficiency of the relational database model, which quickly emerged as my go-to approach for data management in no-code applications.

The world of databases explained

Before we delve into the workings and merits of relational databases, let's cast a brief glance at the broader landscape of databases. Essentially, databases come in several forms:

1. **Flat-file databases:** These are the simplest types of databases where all data is stored in a single table, much like a spreadsheet. They are easy to understand but quickly become inefficient as the volume and complexity of data increases.

2. **Hierarchical databases:** As the name suggests, these databases are structured like a tree, with data arranged in a hierarchy of one-to-many relationships. While they work well for clearly hierarchical data, they struggle with complex, interconnected relationships.

3. **Network databases:** These are an evolution of hierarchical databases and allow many-to-many relationships. However, they are complex and require significant overhead to maintain.

4. **Object-oriented databases:** These store data as objects, like in object-oriented programming. They can handle complex data and relationships but have a steep learning curve and may not fit all use cases.

5. **Relational databases:** These databases store data in tables and use common attributes to link related data across tables. They offer a balance of simplicity,

flexibility, and efficiency, making them the most popular type of database today.

The ascendancy of relational databases

The relational model, proposed by E.F. Codd in 1970, revolutionized the way we think about databases. Unlike its predecessors, the relational database didn't require developers to determine all relationships and data pathways upfront. It allowed a level of flexibility and dynamism that made it ideal for a wide range of applications.

In my experience, this was the key factor that set relational databases apart. When I was a novice, I didn't always know what data I needed, how it was related, and how I might need to use it in the future. This is a common challenge for no-code developers, who often start with a simple idea and gradually uncover its complexity as they build. The relational model, with its ability to efficiently handle changes and expansions in data and relationships, proved to be an invaluable ally.

Relational databases: A closer look

A relational database is like a bustling city of data. Each table in the database is like a building, housing-related pieces of information. The rows in these tables are like the residents, each with its unique identifiers (primary keys), and the columns are like their characteristics.

What makes this city truly function, though, are the relationships between the residents of different buildings. These are formed through shared attributes (foreign keys) that link records across tables. For instance, an 'Orders' table might hold a 'Customer ID' that matches a 'Customer ID' in a 'Customers' table, creating a relationship between a specific order and a specific customer. These relationships enable the database to assemble coherent and meaningful information from disparate data points.

Understanding relationships in a relational database

One of the most important concepts in a relational database is the idea of 'relationships'. In database terms, a relationship is the way in which two or more tables are linked together. The relationship is formed using a key, which is a piece of data that uniquely identifies a record in a table. The key is used to establish a link between the corresponding records in different tables.

There are three types of relationships in relational databases:

1. **One-to-one (1:1):** This type of relationship means that a record in one table is related to only one record in another table. For instance, in a database for a company, you might have an Employees table and a Details table. Each employee has one record in the Details table, containing additional information like their social security number, which is unique for each employee. This is a one-to-one relationship.

2. **One-to-many (1:M):** This is the most common type of relationship. It means that a record in one table can be related to one or more records in another table. For example, consider a Customer table and an Orders table in an e-commerce database. Each customer can make many orders, but each order is made by one customer. Thus, there is a one-to-many relationship between Customers and Orders.

3. **Many-to-many (M:M):** In a many-to-many relationship, a record in one table can be related to one or more records in another table and vice versa. Because this can get quite complicated, it is often managed

by creating a third table, called a junction table or a linking table. For example, consider a Books table and an Author's table in a database for a library. A book might have multiple authors, and an author might write multiple books. This creates a many-to-many relationship, which can be managed with a third table, perhaps called BookAuthors.

Understanding these relationships and how to implement them in your database is crucial, as they are the building blocks of relational databases. These relationships enable the robust and flexible nature of relational databases that can cater to complex and interrelated data requirements. As you get more comfortable with relational databases, you'll find yourself better equipped to handle the data needs of your no-code applications, allowing you to create more complex and powerful solutions.

Understanding through practice: The power of Airtable

When I first started exploring databases, I found the theory intimidating and abstract. The turning point came when I began to use Airtable, a platform that combines the simplicity of spreadsheets with the power of relational databases. Airtable allowed me to build and manipulate databases with a user-friendly interface and visualize the relationships between different sets of data, something that was invaluable in building my understanding.

I spent countless hours creating different tables, establishing relations, viewing data from various perspectives, and trying out complex queries. With each experiment, the concepts of primary keys, foreign keys, relations, and normalization started making more sense. I realized that creating a database is not a task to be taken lightly – it's like laying the foundation of a building; the stronger it is, the more robust your application will be.

Choosing the right database for your needs

When choosing the type of database to use, it is important to consider the nature of your data and the needs of your application. If your data is simple, without many relationships or complex queries, a flat-file database might suffice. However, as soon as you start dealing with complex, interrelated data, the benefits of a relational database become evident.

For example, suppose you are building a simple contact management system where each contact is independent, with no relationships between them. In that case, a flat-file database might suffice. But if you are building an e-commerce app where customers have orders, orders contain products, and products have categories and suppliers, a relational database is a must. It will allow you to manage these complex relationships efficiently and ensure data integrity.

The superiority of the relational model

There are a few reasons why relational databases are considered superior for most applications:

1. **Simplicity:** Despite their ability to handle complex relationships, relational databases are simple to understand and use. The concept of tables, rows, and columns is something we are all familiar with, making it easier to design and manage the database.

2. **Flexibility:** With relational databases, you can add, remove, or modify data without affecting other data sets or needing to restructure your entire database. You can also create views to present data in different ways, without altering the underlying data.

3. **Scalability:** Relational databases can handle a large amount of data and users. They are designed to maintain performance as the database grows.

4. **Data integrity:** In a relational database, data is not duplicated unnecessarily. This reduces the risk of inconsistencies and errors. Built-in rules and

constraints also ensure that the data entered into the database is valid and consistent.

5. **Powerful query capabilities:** SQL (Structured Query Language), the standard language for interacting with relational databases, is powerful and flexible. It allows for complex queries to extract valuable insights from your data.

While it might seem intimidating at first, a hands-on approach to learning, such as tinkering with a tool like Airtable, can demystify the concept. As your understanding grows, so will your ability to use relational databases to power increasingly complex applications, paving the way for a fulfilling and creative journey in no-code development.

Let's take a look at how we could build a relational database for StartRight. First, let's make a rough note of the data that we would need to collect.

1. The startup signs up with their name, email, business sector, year founded, startup bio, and logo.

2. The expert signs up with their name, email, skill set, bio, profile photo, and years of experience.

3. The expert lists a service which has a title, a featured image, a description, and price.

4. The startup makes an order that is linked to the expert.

5. Each order has a chat with a message associated between the startup and the expert.

We could add other data streams here as we grow, such as booking a time and date for a meeting or online courses.

After I have created my rough notes, I like to move on to creating a full data map. This is the definitive list of tables and fields that I need in my database. I like to do this in either a program called Notion.so or in a spreadsheet. This is because I check each one off as I add it to my actual database.

Below is my database structure or map.

User table

Our user table will be a collection of all users, both founders and experts. Because we store the information about each, including their login details, we will keep them in one table. We can distinguish who is a founder and who is an expert by defining a profile type. We'll using something called an option set to define those choices. I'll talk a little more about option sets and what they are later in this section.

- Name
- About
- Profile photo
- Profile type – Linked to Profile Type Option Set (Either Founder or an Expert)
- Skill categories – Category list

Most no-code tools have an email and password field by default. The email, as a unique identifier, will be our Primary Key.

Business details

Our Business Details table will include the business information of both our founders and our experts. We link their user details (which includes whether they are an expert or a founder) by using a relationship to the Business table.

- Business ID (Primary Key)
- Business Name
- Business Logo
- Long Description
- Business Category
- **USER** email (Foreign Key)

Product

Our Business table will be linked only to experts, as they will be creating products and services to sell to our founders. We'll link back to our expert by using their Business ID from the Business Details table.

- Product ID (Primary Key)
- Title
- Short Description
- Long Description
- Featured Image
- Category – Linked to Category Option Set
- Price
- Images (List)
- USER ID (Foreign Key)

Order

The Order table will be linked only to founders, who will be purchasing products and services from our experts. We link each order by linking it back to our User table.

- Order ID (Primary Key)
- **PRODUCT** Product ID (Foreign Key)
- **USER (Founder)** Email (Foreign Key)
- Order Status – Linked to Option Set List (default set as 'ordered')

Reviews

The Review table is where our founder's reviews will be stored. We link each review back to the founder using a link to the User table.

- Review ID (Primary Key)

- Content
- Rating
- **USER** Email (Foreign Key)
- **ORDER** Order ID (Foreign Key)

Chat

All users, both founders and experts, will be able to chat with each other when a sale has been made. We link those individuals to our Users table.

- Chat ID (Primary Key)
- **USERS** Email – List of Users (Foreign Key)

Message

Each message sent will belong to a chat. Whenever a new message is submitted, it will be linked to the Chat table.

- Message ID
- Content
- **CHAT** Chat ID

Primary and Foreign Keys are the links that connects are different tables together so that we can share data back and forth.

Primary Key refers to the unique identifier for each row. For example, imagine we had two experts in our database (each taking up a row) who both created a product with the exact same details, such as 'Social Media Marketing Consultation'. If we wanted to display just one of those items in our app, how would it know which one we wanted? Instead, whenever a new product is added to the database, we create an instruction for our database to generate a unique, random Product ID. That way, when we want a particular product, we just have to call on that Product ID.

Foreign key relates to the Primary Key from another table. Imagine we had all of these wonderful products sitting in our database, but we didn't know who they belonged to.

How would we display accurate information to our founders? How would we be able to pay our experts once a sale had been made? We not only want to link it back to the expert owner, but also display all the relevant information about their business. Because we know that John's Business ID is a Primary Key in the Business table, we connect that information in the Product table. That means that because the two tables (Product and Business) are connected via John's Business ID, we can share data from those tables between each other. Likewise, the Business table is also connected to John's details in the User table, so we're able to link his personal details, such as name and profile photo to each of his products.

PK: Primary Key   FK: Foreign Key

Business Table

Business ID (PK)	Business Name	Logo	User
65791233	John Smith Marketing		John@email.com

Product Table

Product ID (PK)	Title	Business ID (FK)
65790281	Social Media Marketing Consultation	65791233

Figure 5.1 Primary Key

You may also come across the term 'Option Sets'. An Option Set allows you to set pre-determined fields in your database. For example, when an expert signs up, we want them to choose what skills they are really good at. We don't want them to be able to write and add their own skills to our database; that would create an awful mess and make it really difficult for our startups to find the best people possible. Instead, we want to display a list of skills that we have already chosen and allow them to simply select the ones they want.

We create Option Sets for all of the fields where we need to create a list of pre-defined choices.

Profile types

- Startup
- Expert

Categories

- Technology
- Finance
- Investment
- Product
- Design
- Marketing
- Sales

Order status

- Ordered
- In-progress
- Complete

Popular no-code databases on the market

Google Sheets

Google Sheets, a part of the Google Suite, is a popular spreadsheet program that can be used as a simple database for your no-code applications. Unlike a traditional database, Google Sheets is easy to use and requires no prior knowledge of SQL or other database languages.

A Google Sheet consists of individual cells organized in rows and columns. Each row in the spreadsheet can represent a record, and each column can represent a field of that record. For example, if you're building an app to track inventory, each row could represent an item in your inventory, and the columns could be 'Item Name', 'Quantity', 'Price', and so on.

You can create relationships between different sheets (similar to tables in a traditional database) using functions like VLOOKUP and HLOOKUP. For example, you might have a sheet for 'Customers' and another for 'Orders'. You can use these functions to connect the two sheets and retrieve customer information for each order.

One of the advantages of using Google Sheets as a database is its easy integration with many no-code app builders like AppSheet, Glide, and Stacker. These platforms can directly read the data from your Google Sheets and use it to populate your app. Any changes you make in the app will be reflected in the Sheet, and vice versa.

The simplicity and ease of use make Google Sheets a great database option for straightforward no-code applications, like simple CRMs, project management tools, and more.

Airtable

Airtable, on the other hand, is a more powerful tool that combines the simplicity of a spreadsheet with the robustness of a relational database.

In Airtable, you work with bases. Each base is like a mini database that consists of multiple tables. Within each table, you have records (rows) and fields (columns). Each record has a unique record ID, and the fields can be of different types, such as text, number, date, checkbox, attachment, and even a reference to a record in another table (which makes the relational aspect).

One of the major strengths of Airtable is its ability to create and manage relationships between tables, making it more suitable for complex projects that require relational databases. For instance, if you're building a task management app, you could have a table for 'Tasks', and another for 'Users', and create a relationship between them to assign tasks to users.

Airtable also provides a powerful API, enabling it to easily integrate with no-code tools like Zapier, Integromat, or even the front-end builders like Adalo, Bubble, etc. The API allows you to interact with the data in your bases programmatically, enabling automated workflows and synchronizing data across different platforms.

Airtable's user-friendly interface, combined with its powerful features, makes it an excellent choice for no-code applications that need more complexity and relational data structure, like complex project management apps, resource booking apps, and content calendars.

Both Google Sheets and Airtable have their strengths and are powerful in their ways. Depending on the complexity and requirements of your no-code application, you can choose the one that fits your needs best. Remember, the key is to understand your data and the relationships between them and choose the tool that can best handle those relationships.

Bubble's database

Bubble is a comprehensive no-code platform that not only offers front-end development but also a built-in, robust back-end system. Bubble's database structure works in a relational model, offering users the ability to create data types (similar to tables in a traditional database) and fields within them.

An excellent feature of Bubble's database is that it's completely integrated with the app's front-end, meaning you can easily bind database content to the public-facing elements on the screen. This seamless integration simplifies the app development process significantly.

Bubble's database also supports complex relational data structures, making it suitable for building comprehensive applications with intricate relationships between different types of data.

Webflow's CMS

Webflow's built-in database is known as a CMS (Content Management System). The Webflow CMS lets you define content structures known as Collections (akin to database tables). Each Collection can have different fields, like text, images, references to other collections, and more.

Webflow's CMS is particularly strong in developing content-driven websites or applications like blogs, portfolios, news sites, etc., given its rich content management capabilities.

Adalo's database

Adalo is another no-code platform providing both front-end development and a back-end database. In Adalo, you can define Collections for your data with fields that include text, numbers, images, relationships, and more.

Adalo's database is extremely user-friendly and has an intuitive interface, making it a good option for beginners in the no-code space. Moreover, the close integration between the database and the front-end builder simplifies the app-building process.

Building Willo.Social version 1.0 in Airtable

When I built version 1.0 of Willo.Social I used Airtable as my database. I chose it because it was incredibly flexible and integrated with a tonne of no-code app builders. I also liked that it had numerous plugins that could help me automate simple tasks.

In the early days, the idea of Willo.Social was a way for women with hormone conditions to connect with each other locally for shared fitness and social fun. I wanted my users to be able to register, create activities and join activities held by other local members. I created no less than five versions of my first database, feeling at times, completely overwhelmed by even the mention of the word 'database'. But if you plan carefully, it's actually not as hard as it seems.

In this case, my collections were:

- Users (username, avatar, address, email, list of symptoms, list of interested activities)

- User activities (activity name, description, address, date, time, owner)

- Activity sign-ups (member attended, approved (yes or no))

- Messages (sender, message, time, date)

I used relationships to connect this groups of information together.

This exercise was not without a lot of learning. You will come across many data types and equations that you can add to your tables. Some of these are self-explanatory, whilst others left me googling for hours on end. Some of the most common you will come across are:

1. **nteger:** This data type is used to store numeric values without decimal points. Example: age, number of items, etc.

2. **Float/Double:** These data types are used to store numerical values with decimal points. Example: price, weight, etc.

3. **Boolean:** This data type is used to store true or false values.

4. **Char/Varchar:** These are used to store alphanumeric characters. Char is used for fixed length and Varchar is used for variable length characters. Example: names, addresses, etc.

5. **Date/time:** These data types are used to store date and time information. Example: date of birth, event date, etc.

6. **Blob/binary:** These are used to store binary data like images, audio files, etc.

7. **Text/long text:** These data types are used to store long alphanumeric characters. They're usually used for descriptions, comments, etc.

Activity: Map out your data

Spend some time mapping out the data you will need for your app. You can do this with pen and paper, a spreadsheet or a tool like Notion. Write the collection title, followed by all the data points you need to collect. Try having a go at marking where your relations are formed.

6

Building the front-end

What is the front-end?

In traditional software development, the front-end is the part of a software application that users interact with directly, i.e., the buttons, forms, images, blocks of text, etc. Front-end development, therefore, involves creating and implementing all these visual and interactive elements. It requires a keen understanding of both design principles and coding. Front-end developers use programming languages like HTML, CSS, and JavaScript to bring the design and interface of an application to life. They're responsible for everything you see and interact with on a website or application – the layout, the fonts, colours, buttons, images, forms, and any visual transitions or animations.

If you were hiring a professional team to build your app, you might work with both a front-end developer and a back-end developer. Sometimes you may work with someone known as a full-stack developer. This special human is a hybrid of both front-end and back-end developer roles. They are knowledgeable and proficient in both client-side and server-side development and can create a complete application, working on both the visuals that the user interacts with and the data processing that happens behind the scenes.

Now, let's shift gears and delve into the realm of no-code development. In this context, the front-end is still what the end user interacts with, but the process of creating it is quite different.

In no-code development, front-end development is often accomplished through a visual builder. This user-friendly interface allows you to design your application using drag-and-drop functionality and pre-made elements. This eliminates the need for writing actual code and makes the development process far more accessible. Elements like buttons, forms, text fields, images, and even more complex components can be arranged on a page and customized to suit the application's design.

Front-end development in no-code tools doesn't require knowledge of HTML, CSS, or JavaScript. Instead, you use the tool's interface to construct your application visually. You select and place components, change their properties, and define their interactions and behaviours directly within the tool. Even complex functionalities like conditional visibility and dynamic data loading can be defined without writing a single line of code.

In essence, no-code tools have democratized front-end development, making it accessible to anyone, irrespective of their technical background. The only prerequisites are understanding the logic of how applications work and having a clear vision of what you want to create.

I'm most comfortable working with the front end as a graphic designer. I spent much of my early career designing full website layouts and user experiences before turning my hand to HTML and CSS. However, I love the ease of no-code front-end tools. The ability to drag a button and snap it into place is somewhat pleasing. There is no need for me to delve into the CSS files to change the colour or font; I simply click on the property editor and make the changes there and then.

If you have design experience, you could if you wish, spend some time using tools like Figma or Adobe XD to design your app. Although you'll be using drag-and-drop properties, I sometimes find it easier to have a design in mind before I begin building. If you're not a designer, you could press straight ahead or find some free design templates online. If you head over to https://nocodestartup.co, we've listed some of our favourite free design templates for you to use. Some no-tool apps, like Glide, don't offer tonnes of design flexibility, so make sure you can see what you can do with your chosen builder first.

Native app, web, or progressive?

As you begin to design your MVP, one of the pivotal decisions you'll encounter is the choice between building a native app, a web app, or a progressive web app. This is not merely a technical decision but one that also involves considering user experience, development costs, speed to market, and compatibility with various devices. Let's dive deep into understanding what each of these types of applications are, their pros and cons, and how they can fit into the landscape of your MVP.

Native apps

Native applications are software programs developed for use on a specific platform or device, like iOS or Android. They are 'native' because they are written in a programming language that is native to the specific platform they're developed for. This might be Swift or Objective-C for iOS, and Java or Kotlin for Android.

Pros: Native apps deliver the best performance, as they're specifically designed for the platform they're on. They can fully leverage the device's capabilities, accessing hardware features such as the camera, accelerometer, or push notifications. Native apps also offer the best user experience, as they conform to the design guidelines and standards of the platform they're developed for, providing a familiar look and feel for users.

Cons: The main downside of native apps is the cost and complexity of development. Because they are platform-specific, you'll need to develop and maintain separate codebases for each platform, doubling the work to target both iOS and Android. Also, getting your app approved and published on app stores can be a time-consuming process.

Web apps

Web applications, in contrast, are accessible through the internet on a browser. They're written in languages such as HTML, CSS, and JavaScript and are hosted on a server. They're platform-independent, which means they can run on any device with a web browser.

Pros: Web apps are easier and quicker to develop than native apps, as they require only one codebase that works across different platforms. They're also easier to update, as changes are made directly on the server and instantly available to all users. Web apps don't need to go through app store approval processes, providing more control over your app's release and updates.

Cons: Web apps, however, can't leverage hardware capabilities to the same extent as native apps. They also may not offer as smooth or intuitive a user experience, as they don't adhere to the design standards of specific platforms. Additionally, their performance is dependent on the internet connection and can be slower than native apps.

Progressive web apps

Progressive web apps (PWAs) are an innovative type of web app that brings together the best of web and native apps. They are built and delivered through the web but can offer functionalities traditionally available only to native apps, like offline working, push notifications, and access to device hardware.

Pros: PWAs can be installed on the user's device and run offline, offering a near-native app experience while retaining the cross-platform compatibility and easy maintenance of web apps. They also bypass the need for app store approvals.

Cons: PWAs, while powerful, may not support all features of a platform compared to a native app. Also, on iOS, there are restrictions and certain features, like push notifications, are not fully supported.

Choosing the right approach

When I embarked on my journey with Willo.Social, I initially dreamed of it being a native mobile app. Native apps often carry a perception of being more sophisticated and are more in line with consumer trends. However, it's essential to keep an open mind and focus on the core objectives of your MVP: validating your assumptions and learning about your users as quickly and cost-effectively as possible.

I found that many of my users were over the age of 70, and they generally preferred using a desktop over a mobile app. With these user preferences in mind, as well as the simplicity, cost-effectiveness, and readily deployable nature of web apps, I decided to build Willo.Social's MVP as a web app that was mobile responsive. This decision helped expedite our route to market, keeping costs low and allowing us to start collecting valuable user feedback swiftly.

You may have heard of something called 'responsive' design. It refers to the practice of designing a website or app so that its layout, images, and functionalities adjust smoothly to fit various screen sizes. With a responsive design, users get an optimal viewing experience – easy reading and navigation with minimal resizing, panning, or scrolling – regardless of whether they're accessing your app from a desktop, a laptop, a tablet, or a mobile phone.

It's worth noting that while web apps – and, by extension, PWAs – offer broader device compatibility, they aren't necessarily inferior to native apps. Each type of app comes with its strengths and weaknesses, and the choice between them depends on factors such as your specific project requirements, budget, target audience, and desired time to market.

For example, if your app idea heavily relies on using device-specific features, such as a gyroscope or a camera, then a native app would be a better fit. Alternatively, if you're looking for a fast and cost-effective way to reach the widest possible audience, a responsive web app would make sense. And if you need some device capabilities but also want the cost advantages of a web app, a PWA could strike the right balance.

One of the key takeaways from this discussion is that the choice of app type isn't a binary or permanent decision. Many successful products start as simple, single-platform apps – be it native or web – and evolve over time. As your user base grows and your concept gets validated, you can invest more resources into expanding your product, tailoring it to the platforms and devices your users prefer.

The ultimate goal isn't to build the most advanced or trendy app but rather to create a product that effectively meets your users' needs and provides a smooth, enjoyable user experience. Understanding these app types and their pros and cons is the first step in this process.

Remember, the beauty of the no-code movement is that it democratizes software development, allowing entrepreneurs to build, test, and iterate their ideas without breaking the bank or getting lost in the intricacies of code. So, regardless of the route you choose, you can rest assured that there are no-code tools out there that can turn your vision into a functional, user-friendly app.

Types of no-code front-end tools and what they do

When it comes to choosing a no-code front-end design tool there are many options, each with their own pros and cons. What you decide upon really is defined by what level of control you need over your design, as well as what kind of functionality it provides for you.

Some of the most popular types of front-end tools include:

1. **Website builders:** These tools allow users to create websites without needing to write any code. They typically offer drag-and-drop interfaces, templates, and modules for various website functions. Examples include Wix, Squarespace, and Weebly.

2. **App builders:** These tools allow users to create mobile apps with no coding required. They often include templates for common types of apps, and they may allow for custom functionality through integrations or plugins. Examples include Bubble, Adalo, and Appy Pie.

3. **Landing page builders:** These tools specialize in creating landing pages, which are typically single-page websites designed for a specific marketing campaign. They often include features for testing different versions of a page to see which performs better. Examples include Unbounce, Leadpages, and Instapage.

4. **Form builders:** These tools allow users to create web forms for collecting information from users. They can often integrate with other tools for managing and analyzing the collected data. Examples include Typeform, Google Forms, and Formstack.

5. **E-commerce builders:** These tools allow users to create online stores, complete with product listings, shopping carts, and payment processing. Examples include Shopify, BigCommerce, and Magento.

6. **Content management systems (CMS):** These tools allow users to manage and publish content on a website without needing to write code. Examples include WordPress, Drupal, and Joomla.

When I was setting out to build Willo.Social, I knew that I was building a fairly complex app that required a lot of functionality and pages. As a designer, I wanted a high level of control over how my front-end looked. That's why I chose Bubble as my front-end (and back-end) of choice. However, I have a friend who only needed to display pre-formatted graphs and text. He chose a simple template-based system that required very little design but was perfect for his needs and that of his customer.

Connecting the front-end to the back-end

In the world of application development, understanding how data flows between the front end (user interface) and back-end (database) is paramount. This is the heart of how applications work, from the simplest of task management tools to the most complex social media platforms. As we delve deeper into this chapter, we're going to focus on the essential mechanics of creating or fetching data on the front-end, and how it is effectively processed and stored in the back end.

Before we go any further, it's crucial to understand that the methods of data flow vary depending on the type of application builder you're using. If you're working with an application builder that has an in-built database – like Bubble, Adalo, or OutSystems – the connection between the front end and back end is usually automatically managed. That means you do not need to manually connect them, as the tools are designed to handle this seamlessly.

However, if you are working with a no-code builder that requires a connection to a separate external database – like Google Sheets or Airtable – you'll have to follow specific steps to establish this connection. One common method of connecting these databases is through an Application Programming Interface (API). An API serves as a bridge between different software components, allowing them to communicate and share data effectively. I will cover APIs in more depth in an upcoming chapter, but for now, it's enough to know that APIs are essentially the couriers of the digital world – they deliver your request to the provider you're requesting it from and then deliver the response back to you.

In most cases, establishing an API connection is as simple as grabbing your API key from your database account's admin settings and pasting it into the required form on your app builder. The API key serves as a unique identifier that authorizes and validates the interactions between the different software applications.

Once you've established this front-end and back-end connection, the next step is understanding workflows. Workflows are a series of steps or operations that describe how tasks are completed in your application. They define the interaction between the user interface and the database, representing the business logic of your application. In other words, they are the instructions that you give to your app about what to do when a user interacts with it in a particular way.

To illustrate this, let's consider an example using Bubble, a popular no-code tool. Let's say you've designed a user registration form with fields for name and email on your application's front end. To ensure that the data entered into these fields is captured and stored in the database, you would create a workflow. This workflow would specify that when the form is submitted, a new row should be created in the 'Users' table of your database, with the given name and email saved in their respective columns.

Of course, workflows are not limited to such straightforward actions. They can encompass various logic operations, such as conditional statements ('if-else' statements) or more complex sequences of actions. For instance, a more advanced workflow could involve displaying images in a gallery based on the user's preferences or previous interactions.

Every application builder offers different types of workflows, each with its own level of complexity and flexibility. It is essential to get familiar with the specific workflow functionalities of the tool you're using, as this will allow you to manipulate the data flow more effectively.

Digging deeper into workflows

A crucial aspect of workflows is the application of logic, or more specifically, conditional statements. These conditional statements are the bedrock of interactivity in your application – they allow your app to react in different ways depending on the user's input or specific conditions. Now, we'll delve deeper into this subject, exploring the common types of conditional statements and how they can be utilized in no-code development.

'If' statements

'If' statements are the simplest form of conditional logic. They work by evaluating a condition – if the condition is true, the action or a series of actions is executed. If the condition is not met, then the action is ignored.

Let's consider, as an example, that you have a subscription form for a newsletter in your application. You could create an 'if' statement in the workflow like this:

> *'If the email field is not empty when the submit button is clicked, then create a new entry in the subscribers' database'.*

This ensures that no blank entries will be saved in your database.

'If-else' statements

'If-else' statements are a tad more complex. They enable your application to choose between two courses of action depending on whether a certain condition is met. In essence, an 'if-else' statement says:

'If this condition is true, perform this action; otherwise, perform this other action'.

Continuing with our newsletter example, an 'if-else' statement could be: 'If the email field is not empty when the submit button is clicked, then create a new entry in the subscribers' database. Else, display a pop-up message saying, 'Please enter a valid email address'. This way, the user is given feedback when they try to submit an empty form, enhancing the user experience.

'Else-if' statements

'Else-if' statements come into play when you have multiple conditions to check. They are essentially a series of 'if' statements, where each subsequent 'if' is checked only if all previous conditions have been false.

For example, imagine you have a form in your app where users can sign up as either a student, a teacher, or an administrator. Each user type might require a different kind of processing or might be added to a different table in your database. An 'else-if' statement can handle this situation effectively:

'If the selected user type is "student", create a new entry in the "Students" table. Else if the user type is "teacher", create a new entry in the "Teachers" table. Else if the user type is "administrator", create a new entry in the "Administrators" table.'

These types of conditional statements become more and more crucial as your application grows in complexity. They allow your app to handle a multitude of scenarios and cater to different user interactions, making your app more dynamic and robust.

As you dive deeper into the world of no-code, you'll encounter these logic structures frequently. Understanding them is a steppingstone to creating powerful, interactive applications that can handle complex tasks and adapt to your users' needs.

Navigating the world of front- and back-end connections might seem daunting initially, especially when APIs and workflows come into play. However, as you begin to experiment, practice, and build, these concepts will become much more intuitive. Remember, each app builder and each database tool have their pros and cons, and part of the journey is figuring out which one aligns best with your vision, skill level, and project requirements.

Activity: Build a user form with a photo upload field

Building upon our foundational understanding of front-end and back-end, APIs, and workflows, let's advance to the next level by adding a bit more complexity: an image upload feature. In this exercise, you will create a user registration form that allows users to add a profile photo in addition to their name and email. The principles you'll use here expand upon what you've learned so far, adding another layer of functionality to your repertoire.

Step 1: Select your no-code app builder

First, decide on the no-code app builder you would like to use. Glide, Softr, and Bubble remain our recommended options for this exercise. Glide and Softr provide an excellent starting point for beginners due to their user-friendly interfaces. However, Bubble's advanced functionality might appeal to those seeking a more challenging experience.

Step 2: Start a new project

After deciding on your tool, initiate a new project. Typically, this involves navigating to your dashboard, selecting a

'New Project' or 'Start Building' button, and following the subsequent prompts.

Step 3: Design the user form

Now, it's time to design your user form. For this task, create a form with three fields: name, email, and a file upload field for the profile photo. Keep in mind that the design process might vary slightly depending on the tool you've chosen. However, most platforms offer intuitive, drag-and-drop editors for creating form fields.

Step 4: Connect the form to a database

With your user form ready, the next step is linking it to a database. If you're using Glide or Softr, you'll connect the app directly to a Google Sheets document. Each field of the form will correspond to a column in the spreadsheet.

For those using Bubble with its in-built database, you'll create a new data type, such as 'User', and define the fields to match the input fields in your form: 'Name', 'Email', and 'Profile Photo'. Note that for storing images, you should specify the field type as 'image' or 'file', depending on the options available.

Step 5: Create your workflow

The final step in connecting your user form and database is setting up a workflow. This workflow will create a new entry in the database each time a user submits the form.

In Glide and Softr, this generally involves mapping each form field to the respective column in the Google Sheets document.

If you're using Bubble, you'll navigate to the workflow editor, create a new workflow event for when the form is submitted, and then create a new 'User' entry with the inputted data saved in the corresponding fields.

Remember to set up the image upload field so that the uploaded image gets stored in the 'Profile Photo' field (or whatever you have named it) in your database.

Once everything is set up, it's time for testing. Fill out the form, submit it, and then check your database. If all has gone well, the information you inputted, along with the profile photo, should appear as a new entry in your database.

Don't be disheartened if you encounter issues along the way. Debugging and refining are integral parts of the process. This exercise provides a deeper look into the world of no-code development, and there's plenty more to learn and explore as you continue to build!

7

Automations

What are automations?

If you had a go at building a user sign-up form in the previous chapter, then you've already worked with automations. That is, when a user signs up, you have instructed the application to add a new row in a database and add data to it. Pretty cool! However, adding a user to a database isn't going to change the world. Thankfully though, automations can get a lot more exciting and complex!

Reflecting on my personal journey in the realm of software development, one of the crucial turning points was my encounter with the concept of connecting data sources to provide an even higher level of functionality (and problem-solving). Some years ago, I embarked on a personal project: a menu planner. I was passionate about fitness and healthy eating, and I sought to create a tool to help track my weight and generate new recipe recommendations.

At the time, I had developed a basic website that allowed me to input my weight. However, to find the recipes, I had to navigate to a separate website, input various parameters each time, and sift through a plethora of options before I found something that suited my dietary needs and preferences. This process was both tedious and time-consuming – it felt like a chore rather than the exciting venture I had envisioned.

One day, in a casual conversation, I mentioned my struggles to an acquaintance. They responded with a simple, life-altering suggestion, 'Why don't you just automate it with an API call?'

API, a term I had previously encountered, was a vague concept to me. My understanding was that it was akin to a handshake between software systems, enabling them to exchange data. Many companies offer APIs – some for free (or open source), others charging a nominal fee per data transfer. The recipe website I was using did offer an API, but I was clueless about how to transfer data from their database to mine.

This realization marked the start of my deep dive into the world of automations and APIs. APIs became a beacon, guiding me towards a horizon where data could move seamlessly across different platforms. APIs are not just handshakes; they're like interpreters that facilitate dialogues between disparate systems, translating and delivering data in a format that the receiving system can understand.

In no-code development, automations are incredibly potent. Imagine an army of robots doing all of the manual tasks that you hate or which take up too much of your time. An automation is essentially like one of those robots. They facilitate intricate operations, streamline processes, and allow applications to perform complex tasks with little to no human intervention. When implemented correctly, they not only boost efficiency but also significantly enhance the user experience.

For instance, imagine a health and fitness application that not only tracks a user's weight and diet but also integrates with external platforms to pull in personalized exercise routines, offers nutritional advice, and even sends reminders for scheduled workouts – all done automatically.

Services like Zapier, Make, and n8n serve as hubs for automation. They connect disparate apps, facilitate data transfer, and orchestrate automatic workflows, making it possible to automate tasks that would otherwise require significant manual effort. These tools are critical in the no-code universe, as they eliminate the need for coding to facilitate API-based interactions.

Consider a CRM (Customer Relationship Management) application. Automations in such an application could include:

1. **Lead management:** When a visitor fills out a form on a website, an automation can trigger that adds the lead's details into the CRM and sends a follow-up email to the visitor.

2. **Task creation:** If a sales representative updates a lead's status to 'contacted', an automation can create a task for a follow-up call in a week.

3. **Reporting:** At the end of each week, an automation can generate a report detailing the leads contacted, sales made, tasks completed, and more. This report could be emailed directly to the manager.

In each of these examples, automation not only eliminates manual tasks but also reduces the chances of human error and improves efficiency.

Many no-code tools also include built-in automations. For instance, Bubble allows you to automate workflows within your application. You could configure an automation that triggers when a user submits a form – this could create a new database entry, send a confirmation email to the user, or even update another part of your application.

You can easily create actions that happen when a button is clicked or a form is submitted – such as updating user profiles, recording transactions, or sending push notifications.

When we think of automation, it's essential to understand its broader implications. Automation not only makes processes faster and more efficient but also enables us to deliver more personalized experiences to our users. For example, when a user signs up for your application, an automated workflow could trigger a personalized welcome email. Similarly, when a user adds an item to their wishlist or cart, an automated process could recommend related items.

Let's consider Webflow, a no-code platform that allows for automations in website design. With its built-in CMS (Content Management System), you can create an automated workflow to publish a blog post at a scheduled date and time. Additionally, you could automate the process of populating your website's 'related articles' section based on the tags or categories of the current blog post.

Even platforms like Glide and Softr, which primarily utilize Google Sheets as their backend, offer automation possibilities. With Glide, you can create actions that update your Google Sheets data when a user interacts with your app. For example, when a user completes a survey on your Glide app, it could automatically update your Google Sheets database with the new data.

Remember, automation is not about eliminating human interaction – it's about augmenting our abilities, reducing error-prone manual tasks, and letting us focus on what truly matters. Automations are like the backstage crew in a theatre production – they work silently behind the scenes to ensure a seamless performance on stage.

In my case, implementing automation and understanding APIs turned the tide for my menu-planner project. By automating the process of fetching recipes from an external website based on my parameters, I was able to focus on improving the user experience and refining other aspects of my application.

Automations are a game-changer in the world of no-code development. They unlock new avenues of efficiency, reduce manual work, and free you up to focus on the creative and strategic aspects of building your application. Whether it's managing data, connecting to external APIs, scheduling tasks, or enhancing user interactions, automation is a powerful ally in the no-code landscape.

With this understanding of automation, we can explore the intricate layers of no-code development, moving from the basic fundamentals towards a more complex, robust understanding. The world of automation awaits, ready to streamline your journey in the no-code universe.

A deep dive into API's

In the ever-evolving digital world, APIs (Application Programming Interfaces) serve as indispensable connectors that allow various software systems to communicate and exchange information. If we try to imagine this in the simplest of terms, think of an API as a messenger or a courier. In this scenario, you (or one software application) are sending a message or a package (request) to someone (another software application) through a courier (API). The courier (API) takes the package (request) from you and delivers it to the receiver (another software), who in turn sends a response back to you through the same courier (API).

Let's now delve deeper into the action that happens when an API call, or in other words, a request, is made. An API call is essentially what happens when you send a request to a server using the API, and the server returns a response. This process is analogous to you making a phone call to a friend – you (the client application) make a call (API call), and your friend (server) receives the call and responds.

API calls are typically made using HTTP (Hypertext Transfer Protocol) requests, which primarily include four methods: GET, POST, PUT, and DELETE.

GET: This method retrieves data from a server. For instance, if you wanted to obtain a list of all the users registered on your app, you'd use a GET request.

POST: This method sends data to a server to create a new entry. So, when you're registering a new user to your app, you'd use a POST request.

PUT: This method is used to update existing data on a server. Suppose a user wants to change their profile picture on your app; you'd use a PUT request.

DELETE: As the name suggests, this method deletes existing data from a server. If a user wants to delete their account on your app, you will use a DELETE request.

Let's take a look at an example of an API call using JavaScript, making a GET request:

```
fetch('https://website.example.com/items', {
method: 'GET',
})
.then(response => response.json())
.then(data => console.log(data))
.catch((error) => {
 console.error('Error:', error);
});
```

This piece of code sends a GET request to 'https://website.example.com/items'. It then waits for a response, converts that response into a format called JSON (JavaScript Object Notation), and prints the resulting data. If there is any error during this process, it is captured and an error message is printed.

Now, let's understand what JSON is. JSON stands for JavaScript Object Notation. It is a way of representing data that uses the format of JavaScript objects. JSON represents data as key-value pairs.

A key-value pair is a set of two linked data items: a key, which is a unique identifier for some item of data, and the value, which is either the data that is identified or a pointer to the location of that data.

Here's an example of a key-value pair in JSON:

```
{
'firstName': 'John',
'lastName': 'Doe',
'email': 'john.doe@example.com'
```

Here, 'firstName', 'lastName', and 'email' are keys, and 'John', 'Doe', and 'john.doe@example.com' are their respective values. This way of representing data is very simple to read and write and is therefore, widely used in data exchanges via APIs.

When data is sent via an API, it can be encapsulated in a variety of formats, but the most common one is JSON because of its ease of use and compatibility with a wide range of programming languages.

Why would you use APIs in your no-code app?

APIs play a crucial role in the modern application ecosystem, and that includes no-code apps as well. There are several reasons why developers and no-code creators alike choose to leverage APIs in their applications.

1. **Access to external services and data:** APIs provide an efficient way to connect with external services and fetch or send data. For instance, a weather application can use an API to retrieve real-time weather data from a weather data provider. Similarly, an e-commerce no-code app can use APIs to access a payment gateway and handle transactions. The main advantage here is that you do not need to build these services from scratch; you can leverage what's already available, saving time and resources.

2. **Automation:** With APIs, you can automate repetitive tasks. For example, if you have a blog site built with a no-code tool and want to post your articles on multiple platforms (like Medium, LinkedIn, etc.), APIs can automate this process. Once set up, the articles can be simultaneously published on all these platforms, reducing manual work.

3. **Integration:** APIs allow for seamless integration of different software systems. This integration helps create an interconnected digital ecosystem where data flows freely from one system to another. For instance,

you could use APIs to integrate your no-code CRM app with your email marketing tool, allowing you to automate the process of adding new leads to your email campaigns.

4. **Enhanced user experience:** APIs can significantly enhance the user experience of your app by bringing in dynamic content and third-party services. For instance, Google Maps API can be integrated into a no-code app to provide location services, improving the user experience.

5. **Scalability:** APIs can make your no-code apps more scalable. If your app's user base grows and you need to upgrade certain features or add new ones, APIs from third-party services can make this process easier and faster.

6. **Efficiency:** Instead of coding every feature from scratch, APIs allow you to stand on the shoulders of giants by leveraging already developed and tested services. This can significantly speed up the development process, making your work more efficient.

7. **Cost savings:** APIs can provide significant cost savings. By using APIs, you eliminate the need to develop, test, and maintain certain features, reducing the overall development costs.

APIs are essentially superpowers for no-code apps. They allow you to integrate your application with powerful services, automate tasks, enhance the user experience, and scale more efficiently. As a no-code builder, understanding APIs and how to use them can significantly enhance the capabilities of the apps you build.

Retrieving data with a webhook

When building your no-code app, you may come across the term 'webhook'. Webhooks, much like APIs, are fundamental building blocks in the architecture of modern web applications, facilitating efficient communication between different applications.

A webhook, in its simplest form, is a means for one application to provide other applications with real-time information automatically. It's akin to a system of push notifications between websites or web applications, leading to the term 'webhook' – effectively 'hooking' together different web applications with live updates.

Unlike APIs that operate on a request-response model (pull), webhooks work on a push principle. This means data is delivered from the source application to the destination without the destination needing to request it. To illustrate this concept, think about receiving an important email. Instead of frequently refreshing your inbox (which parallels making repeated API calls), you receive a notification as soon as the email arrives (analogous to a webhook). This real-time information exchange is a distinguishing feature of webhooks.

Consider an example where you're creating a no-code e-commerce app. In such an application, it's critical to track whenever a new order comes in. By setting up a webhook, your application can automatically send new order data to a specified endpoint, such as a URL, the instant an order is placed. This data can then initiate other tasks, such as sending a confirmation email to the customer or updating your inventory records.

The crucial difference between APIs and webhooks lies in their data communication models. APIs operate on a request-response mechanism, meaning you ask for the data, and the API responds with it. To get updated data, you need to continually make new requests. In contrast, webhooks automatically transmit data the moment a predefined event occurs – data is 'pushed' to you without any request needed from your side.

Choosing between an API and a webhook

Both webhooks and APIs play significant roles in the development of dynamic and interactive applications. While APIs grant your application access to an extensive range of functions from other services, webhooks ensure your application is constantly updated with real-time data. As a no-code developer, understanding and harnessing both APIs and webhooks will help you create more comprehensive, efficient, and user-friendly applications.

Choosing between using an API and a webhook largely depends on the nature of your application, the kind of data you're dealing with, and how often that data changes or needs to be accessed.

Use an API when:

1. **Data retrieval on demand:** If your application requires data from another service in response to a specific user action, an API is usually the better choice. For example, when a user searches for a book in an online store, an API call can be made to retrieve and display the book details from the database.

2. **Control over request frequency:** APIs operate on a request-response model, so you have total control over when and how frequently requests are made. This is useful if you want to manage the rate of data transfer for efficiency or cost reasons.

3. **Complex queries:** If you need to access specific subsets of data or perform complex queries, APIs are generally more flexible. They often support advanced querying capabilities that allow you to filter, sort, or manipulate the data before it is sent.

Use a webhook when:

1. **Real-time updates:** If your application needs to respond immediately to certain events, webhooks are the better choice. For example, in a chat app, when a user sends a message, a webhook can immediately push the message to the receiver's device.

2. **Automated workflow:** Webhooks are excellent for automating workflows between different services. For example, a webhook could be set up to trigger an email confirmation to a customer whenever a new order is placed.

3. **Reducing server load:** Since webhooks only send data when a specific event happens, they can help reduce the load on your server compared to regularly polling an API for updates.

In practice, many applications make use of both APIs and webhooks to cater to different scenarios. APIs typically handle more diverse and complex tasks, allowing for comprehensive data retrieval and manipulation, while webhooks are instrumental in creating real-time, event-driven functionalities. By understanding their distinct benefits, you can more effectively choose the right tool for your no-code application's needs.

Using AI in your app

The realm of Artificial Intelligence (AI) is an exciting frontier that's rapidly expanding and transforming the way we live, work, and interact. At its core, AI is a branch of computer science that aims to build machines capable of mimicking human intelligence. But in reality, it's much more than that. It's a tool that's pushing the boundaries of what's possible, enabling us to solve complex problems, gain insights from vast amounts of data, and automate tasks to a degree we could only have dreamt of just a few years ago.

AI's versatility is one of its most striking aspects. Today, there's a burgeoning array of AI applications available on the market, each designed to serve a specific purpose. From AI chatbots that can handle customer queries to sophisticated machine learning models that can predict trends and outcomes, the applications of AI are growing every day. There's such a wide variety of AI tools available that it would be impossible to cover them all in this book. However, I can give you a glimpse into the different types of AI models and what they're capable of.

AI models can be broadly categorized based on their capabilities: narrow AI, general AI, and superintelligent AI. Narrow AI, or weak AI, specializes in one specific task. Examples of this include voice recognition systems like Siri and Alexa or recommendation algorithms used by Netflix or Amazon. These systems are brilliant at what they do, but they're limited to their specific tasks.

General AI, on the other hand, possesses the ability to understand, learn, and apply knowledge across a broad range of tasks, much like a human. While this level of AI is mostly theoretical at this point, it represents a significant area of research in the field.

Superintelligent AI takes it a step further. This type of AI would surpass human capabilities in the most economically valuable work. It's an exciting yet daunting concept that's currently more science fiction than reality.

In the current landscape, the most impactful AI models are examples of narrow AI. Among these, language and image processing models like ChatGPT and DALL-E by OpenAI have been revolutionary. ChatGPT, a language model, can generate human-like text, assisting in tasks like idea generation, content creation, or even database schema design. DALL-E, on the other hand, is an image-generating model capable of creating unique visuals based on textual descriptions, serving as a powerful tool for content creators.

The integration of AI tools like ChatGPT and Dall-E into no-code applications can open up a wealth of possibilities, enhancing functionality, enriching user experience, and automating various tasks. Here are some ways you can use these AI models in your no-code applications:

1. **Content generation with ChatGPT:** ChatGPT can generate human-like text based on the prompts given. This can be used in a blogging app where users need help coming up with content. You can set up an API call to ChatGPT to generate a draft based on the user's chosen topic, which the user can then edit and refine.

2. **Customer support with ChatGPT:** If you're building an application that requires customer support, ChatGPT could serve as a first line of support. When users have questions or issues, ChatGPT can provide instant, accurate responses, reducing the burden on human support staff and speeding up resolution times.

3. **Idea generation with ChatGPT:** Suppose you're building a project management or brainstorming app. In that case, you can use ChatGPT to generate new project ideas, solutions to problems, or innovative approaches to tasks based on the user's inputs and requirements.

4. **Visual content generation with Dall-E:** Dall-E can create images from textual descriptions, which can be especially useful in design or social media planning apps. Users can input a description of the image they want, and Dall-E can generate a corresponding visual.

5. **Interactive learning with ChatGPT and Dall-E:** If you're creating an educational app, these AI models could be used to create interactive learning experiences. ChatGPT could be used to answer

students' questions in real-time, while Dall-E could provide visual representations of concepts to help solidify understanding.

6. **Personalized user experience with ChatGPT and Dall-E:** You can also use these AI models to personalize the user experience. For example, ChatGPT can generate personalized content based on user preferences, and Dall-E can create customized visuals that appeal to individual users.

In essence, integrating AI models like ChatGPT and Dall-E into no-code apps can significantly enhance their capabilities, automate tasks, and create a more engaging, personalized experience for users. However, it's essential to bear in mind the ethical considerations and guidelines when using such powerful AI tools, ensuring that they are used responsibly and with respect for users' privacy and data security.

Here are some examples of other AI no-code tools on the market:

1. **DataRobot:** This platform offers many features to help businesses leverage AI quickly and efficiently. It supports both code-first and code-free development of AI/ML (Artificial Intelligence/Machine Learning) projects. The platform also integrates well with tools like GitHub for automated workflows. It allows users to build no-code AI apps directly from a model leaderboard, simplifying the app creation process for people without machine learning experience.

2. **MonkeyLearn:** This tool focuses on text analysis and machine learning. It is designed to make these processes easier, even for those without a deep understanding of AI or machine learning.

3. **MLJAR:** This platform offers automated machine-learning capabilities. While not much detailed

information is available, it's designed to be user-friendly and is highly rated.

4. **Obviously.ai:** This tool is designed to be the fastest and simplest data prediction tool in the world. In less than a minute, you can connect to your favourite data source, make predictions, and share them with your team. It offers a simple three-step process: Add a CSV file or integrate with your data sources, pick your prediction column from a dropdown (the AI will auto-build), and then get a report that shows top drivers, predictions, and simulates 'what-if' scenarios.

5. **Akkio:** Akkio is a simple, visual, easy-to-use platform that allows anyone to utilize the power of AI in their everyday tasks, especially in sales, marketing, and finance. It enables you to train and deploy AI models in under five minutes, with no AI experience needed. Akkio allows any user with a working knowledge of spreadsheets to draw predictive insight from their data and enables proactive decision-making. It also helps automate low-value tasks and empowers even non-technical employees to build hundreds of models in practically no time.

Connecting your app to external data the no-code way

Automation tools have revolutionized the way businesses operate by streamlining processes and tasks, enabling teams to focus on more strategic and creative tasks. In the realm of my projects, Zapier and Make are two such automation tools that have become invaluable. They serve as bridges between different applications and services, automating data transfers and tasks without the need for writing any code. These tools play a pivotal role in connecting no-code AI platforms to other digital tools, opening a world of possibilities for efficient workflows.

Zapier

Zapier shines as a robust online automation tool that integrates with a vast array of popular apps, such as Gmail, Slack, Mailchimp, and many more. It's designed to eliminate the need for repetitive tasks by connecting your favourite apps and automating actions.

Creating an automated workflow in Zapier is straightforward. You craft a 'Zap', which is a command instructing Zapier to perform a certain action when a specific event occurs. A Zap comprises a trigger (the event that initiates the workflow) and one or more actions (the tasks executed following the trigger). For example, if you want to save Gmail attachments to Dropbox automatically, you create a Zap where receiving a new email in Gmail is the trigger, and saving the email's attachment to Dropbox is the action.

Zapier supports over 3,000 applications, creating a broad landscape for automation. Additionally, it provides support for webhooks, enabling the triggering of Zaps from any software capable of sending an HTTP request, further broadening its automation capabilities.

Make

Make stands as another powerful automation tool designed to streamline manual processes through easy-to-configure yet sophisticated features. Like Zapier, Make uses a system of triggers and actions, but it calls these workflows 'Scenarios'.

Despite the similarities, Make offers more complexity in creating Scenarios. Beyond a simple trigger-action chain, you can construct workflows that split based on conditions, loop through data, and handle more nuanced tasks. This added versatility makes Make particularly useful for intricate workflows.

Make directly integrates with a multitude of popular apps and also offers HTTP/SOAP and JSON modules. These features mean Make can integrate with virtually any web service, all without writing a single line of code.

Both Zapier and Make provide a powerful means of connecting no-code AI platforms to other software tools, automating data transfers and actions based on the AI platform's output. As an example, an automation could send data from your CRM to your AI platform, generate a prediction, and then incorporate that prediction back into the CRM – all without any coding. By leveraging these automation tools, businesses can save time, reduce human error, and focus their efforts on tasks that require a human touch.

How I used API's to enhance Willo.Social

When I was building Willo.Social, I realized that our users required an easy way to select a meeting venue from anywhere in the UK and eventually from around the globe. Manually entering millions of different addresses was obviously impractical, if not impossible. This is where Google Places came into the picture.

Google Places is a comprehensive API provided by Google that grants access to a vast database of location data, including commercial addresses, landmarks, and other points of interest. For a growing platform like ours, it was the perfect solution to provide our users with an easy and efficient way to specify their meeting venues.

The development of Willo.Social using the no-code platform Bubble further simplified the process. Bubble offers a Google Places plugin which makes integrating this extensive location database into our app straightforward. Users can now start typing an address, and Google Places will automatically provide a list of possible matches, streamlining the process of specifying a venue for our users.

For those using an app builder that doesn't offer a built-in Google Places plugin, there are tools like Zapier and Make.com that can be used to connect your app to the Google Places API. These tools help to create workflows that integrate your app with the API, making the benefits of Google Places accessible to a wider range of platforms.

The successful integration of Google Places into Willo. Social has made the task of specifying meeting venues quick, accurate, and user-friendly. Through the use of Google's vast location data and the flexibility of no-code platforms, we've been able to implement a complex yet highly beneficial feature that greatly enhances our platform's user experience.

The success with Google Places encouraged us to explore further the potential of integrating powerful third-party services into our app. The next challenge we aimed to address was implementing a reliable and secure payment system. To achieve this, we turned to Stripe, a leading global payment processor known for its robust capabilities and user-friendly interface.

Just like with Google Places, integrating Stripe into our app using Bubble was a seamless process. Bubble offers a Stripe plugin that simplifies the connection, allowing us to incorporate secure payment processing into our app without needing to write a single line of code. The plugin offers access to Stripe's core features, including the ability to set up recurring subscription payments, issue refunds, and manage customer billing information.

For app builders that don't provide a direct Stripe plugin, automation tools like Zapier can bridge the gap. With Zapier, you can set up a workflow that connects your app with Stripe's API, automating payment processing and other related tasks.

The addition of Stripe to our platform has been pivotal in our growth. It has not only allowed us to provide a safe and efficient way for our users to manage their payments but also instilled a sense of trust in our platform. By harnessing the power of no-code platforms and third-party integrations, we've been able to create a comprehensive, user-friendly experience that meets the diverse needs of our user base.

Activity: Create your first automation

Head over to your favourite automation platform (or try both) and try and create simple automation. Below, I have listed some suggestions to get your started.

Connect Gmail to a Google Sheet so that every time someone emails you, you have a record of who contacted you, when, and what they said. Great for keeping track of your contacts.

In the same way, you could connect your Gmail account to a Google Sheet so that when you send an email to someone, it records it in a database with the date and time.

8

Let's build

So what have we covered so far? We have carefully selected a problem based on our customer research. We've asked them all the right questions to understand their pain points. We have an idea in our mind that we believe will solve that problem. We've also created our app user flow and our wireframes which we've let potential users give feedback on. Our data is mapped out so we know exactly how our tables will relate to each other in a database.

Now all we have to do is build. I'm going to get started and build StartRight. I could use many no-code tools to create my marketplace. Let me draw up a list of some options I could use.

- Wordpress: I've used Wordpress for over 15 years so I completely understand how it works. I can use a multi-vendor plugin or marketplace theme to create my marketplace.

- Softr: I've used Softr and I like its drag-and-drop front-end design tool as I want to create a unique look for my site. Softr already has marketplace templates included which already has the database and front-end set up. I would just need to customize it to my liking.

- Sharetribe.com: This tool is built primarily for multi-vendor marketplaces. This could be a great way to get our app up and running in a matter of hours.

- Bubble: My favourite no-code tool. Bubble offers so much flexibility that we could build a great platform to grow upon.

If this was a real-world situation it's highly likely that I would use Sharetribe to get this app up and running. I'd be able to build it really quickly with their point-and-click interface. I'd also be able to test it with my target customers within a very short space of time.

However, I also know that Bubble would give me so much more control over what I could do in the future. Plus, it's a great way to show you how such a tool can be used... so let's go with Bubble! I'm going to take you through four sections of how I would create this idea if I were building in a real-world scenario.

1. Setting up the database

The initial step in our exploration involves organizing our database. To do this, we refer back to our previously devised data map which holds a variety of tables such as 'User', 'Business details', 'Product', 'Order', 'Reviews', and 'Chat', among others. Each of these tables encompasses numerous fields specifically designed to hold different data types like text, image, numerical, or geographic data.

In order to establish relationships among the various tables in our database, we configure foreign keys. As an example, we connect the email field (serving as our primary key) of the User table to the 'Business details' table. This link symbolizes the relationship between a user and their respective businesses. Likewise, we construct similar links for other tables such as 'Product', 'Order', and 'Reviews'. In the realm of Bubble, creating a foreign key is as straightforward as selecting the desired table we wish to establish a link with from our field box.

Within Bubble, our option sets reside in a separate tab. The creation process for these option sets mirrors that of tables, but with a slight difference – here, our option names assume the role of our fields.

If at any point you falter while structuring your database, there's no need to fret. Rest assured; I've invested countless hours in rectifying databases due to various errors and missteps. It's a learning process punctuated with a fair share of trial and error.

For an extensive list of field types, you may come across, feel free to peruse the reference section at the end of this book.

Keep in mind that Bubble has an automated system that creates the email and password fields within our database. Hence, it's not necessary for you to manually create these in your user table.

2. Setting up the user interface

As a designer, this is my favourite part of the app-building experience, and I'm lucky that Bubble has an incredible selection of native and user-created interface elements to choose from.

Looking over the user flow diagram that I created earlier, I look at the path I want my user to follow and jot down the high-level pages I think I will need to create.

1. **Home page:** This is the main landing page where users can search for services, filter services by popular categories, and view popular services within a category.

2. **Registration page:** The bit that actually signs our user up.

3. **Search results page:** This page displays the results of a user's search for services.

4. **Product page:** Showing all available services and products which can be filtered to the user's requirements.

5. **Detailed Product page:** This page provides a detailed view of a specific product or service, including a full description, price, and reviews.

6. **Order review page:** Here, users can review their order before proceeding to checkout.

7. **Checkout page:** This is where users enter their payment information and complete the purchase.

8. **Order management page:** After purchase, users are redirected to this page, where they can manage all of their orders. Freelancers can also view and manage the orders they've received here.

9. **Messaging page:** This page facilitates communication between users. They can switch between different conversations and send messages in real-time.

10. **User settings page:** Users can update their details on this page.

11. **User profile page:** This will list the user-facing details about the user, whether it's a startup or an expert.

12. **Product listing page:** Freelancers can manage all of their services on this page.

13. **About page:** For new users who want to know more about who we are.

A frequent query I encounter is why, given a user base of 100, we don't need to create 100 separate user pages. The answer lies in the dynamic nature of the pages we're crafting. These pages extract and showcase the requisite data from our database, tailored to the specific viewer. Instead of overwhelming our server (which houses all of our app files) with 100 individual user pages, we instruct a single user page to fetch data according to various parameters. This clever trick is achieved in our workflows, which we'll delve into in the next step.

Once our necessary pages have been constructed, the enjoyable phase (at least for me) commences.

Staring at the stark, white expanse of Bubble, I can sense my heart pounding a bit faster and my breaths becoming more rapid. It's akin to an artist facing a blank canvas – that void space is utterly intimidating. If I were to start haphazardly inserting elements at this stage, chances are, the end result wouldn't be aesthetically pleasing nor would it incorporate all the features I truly desire.

But worry not! The wireframes, meticulously designed earlier and validated by potential customers, will now serve as my guide.

Our homepage holds critical significance as it's tasked with enticing both our users and experts to sign up for an account. More crucially, I aspire to offer them an exploratory trial of our site before they commit to signing up. Such an approach increases the chances of them discovering something appealing or necessary, subsequently leading to their onboarding as customers. Certain apps may prefer to keep their internal pages confidential, particularly if it's a B2B tool or an exclusive members community. A vast number of no-code builders provide settings to keep certain pages inaccessible to non-logged-in users. However, for our 'Startright' project, we wish to keep our doors as open as possible.

Upon landing on any website or app, you'll likely encounter a powerful statement or a prominent image. This is known as your hero header or hero image (see Figure 8.1). It serves as your user's initial snapshot of your business and its offerings, so it's crucial to make a compelling first impression. For 'Startright', I envision a bold text headline prominently displayed at the centre of the screen, succinctly stating our mission – 'Hire Experts for Your Startup'. To facilitate immediate engagement, we'll position a search box beneath it, enabling users to begin their exploration using relevant keywords.

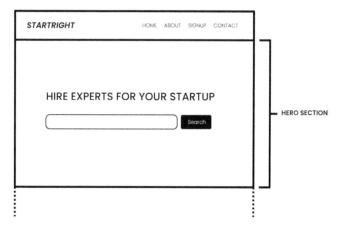

Figure 8.1 Hero header

As I design and arrange the components on my page, I use something called a group (sometimes called a container in some tools) to keep certain elements together. For instance, the top of my app contains a logo and my horizontal menu (see Figure 8.2). I want to group all of these things together so that I can apply certain rules to them, such as how much space I want to add around this group or whether it should be aligned in the centre or not. I can also save these grouped elements and use them on other pages with ease.

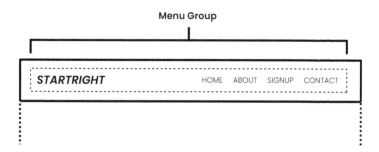

Figure 8.2 Menu group

Beneath our menu, we aim to highlight some of our distinguished experts and the services they provide. In

Bubble, we deploy an element known as a 'repeating group' for this purpose (see Figure 8.3). This is a type of group that allows us to display similar repeating information, such as an experts name and photo.

For each expert, we'll require a text headline to display the service title, an image to portray the service's featured image, paragraph text to present a brief description, and, lastly, text to reveal the service's price. To facilitate immediate action, let's also incorporate a 'buy now' button here. Each of these elements will be dynamically populated for each expert within the repeating group, creating a seamless and visually appealing display.

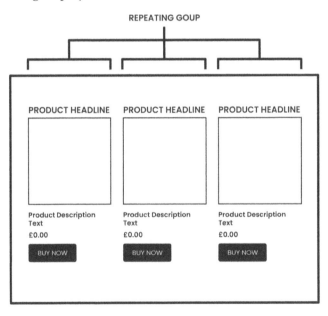

Figure 8.3 Repeating group

Our homepage will also feature sections dedicated to startups, where we outline who we are and why our experts are the ideal solution for their needs. Naturally, we will incorporate a 'sign up' button in this section for easy user access.

Similarly, we will include another section targeting potential experts. While we may consider developing a more detailed page specifically for experts down the line, our immediate objective with the MVP is a swift launch. We can enrich our platform with additional marketing-oriented pages after going live.

Let's also not overlook the importance of the Menu or Navigation bar, which will take precedence over our hero header. This menu is dynamic and will vary based on the viewer's status. For non-logged-in users, the displayed pages will be:

- Home
- Products
- About us
- Sign-up
- Sign-in

Once a user is logged in, my menu will show the following:

- Products
- User profile page (so the user can see their own profile)
- Orders (with a list of open or completed orders)
- User settings
- Sign-out

At a later stage, we'll develop a workflow instructing Bubble on which menu to display in each scenario.

I proceeded to construct the additional pages required. Given this phase can be rather time-consuming (depending on the number of pages needed), focus on creating only the essential pages at the outset. More can be added later.

I ensure our app is responsive by utilizing Bubble's Flexbox system. In essence, I deselect the 'make this website fixed width' option and arrange my layout using rows and columns. Bubble grants you the ability to modify how these rows and columns contract or expand based on screen size. This is achieved by setting your minimum width to 0 and maximum width to 'inf' (infinity). Additionally, a feature known as 'conditions' lets you define the appearance of an element based on browser size. I frequently employ this to adjust text size if a headline appears excessively large on mobile.

3. Creating our workflows

Workflows are sequences of operations that animate our app, generally triggered by a user action such as clicking a registration button. Each no-code tool handles workflows differently, but in Bubble, they resemble the following (see also Figure 8.4):

User Registration:

Upon clicking the 'sign up button' > The user is registered.

Following this, a pop-up emerges displaying the settings for this workflow. This includes the input forms you've incorporated in your sign-up form. Here, you can specify which input field corresponds to which entry in your database.

For instance:

Email = Input > Email's value

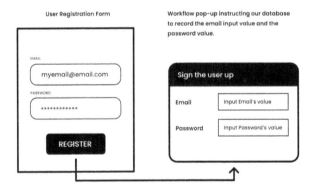

Figure 8.4 Workflow popup

Therefore, the 'email' field in our database will be the email entered in our sign-up form's email field.

The same methodology is applicable to passwords.

Furthermore, we need to input our user's Name and profile image. This can be done by choosing 'Change another field', and subsequently selecting the relevant field and input box.

Adding a new product or service

When an expert introduces a new product or service, we create our container and introduce the requisite form elements like product title, short description, long description, category, featured image, price, and category.

The workflow gets triggered when the expert clicks on the 'submit' button.

Similar to our registration form, we have numerous 'input' elements that allow users to input their text. However, we also include a dropdown box for categories, enabling our experts to select from the predefined skills we set up earlier in our database.

To accomplish this, we click on our dropdown menu input element to access the property editor. We switch from 'static choices' to 'dynamic choices'. Then, for the 'types of choices' option, we choose our 'Categories' option set (see Figure 8.5).

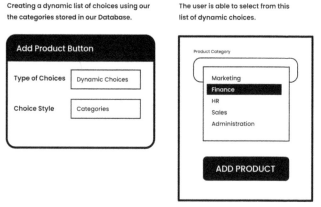

Figure 8.5 Dynamic choices

This process brings forth the options set we've already established in our database, facilitating our expert to make an appropriate selection.

Plugins

As we sign up both a user and an expert, we're interested in their location, ideally their closest city. Bubble offers a range of enhancements to its principal interfaces and tools, which are known as 'Plugins'. These are add-ons created by third-party developers that integrate into your Bubble app to provide additional functionality. Some plugins are available for free, while others carry a cost.

One such plugin is Google Places. Within my sign-up form, I utilize a search input that allows the user to start typing their address. After connecting Google Places to my Google API, the user should see a list of similar addresses pop up, from which they can select the correct one. During our workflow, we configure it such that when the user clicks the 'signup' button, the user's location is reflected as the input value in the location search box.

I approach each page one at a time, incorporating workflows as I progress.

Occasionally, I have to refer to the Bubble documentation to learn how to create a specific workflow, or I might reach out to one of the experts in the Bubble community. It's likely that someone else has already tackled and resolved the task I'm trying to accomplish.

4. Testing

Once I've meticulously designed all of my pages and completed every workflow, I devote the following days to rigorously testing the app using test user data, which I generate myself. This is a crucial step, often overlooked in the rush of development. However, by taking the time to run through each aspect of the application, I can catch and rectify any lurking bugs or functionality issues before they become problematic for real users. This process can be likened to a dress rehearsal before a performance, ensuring that everything is in order and running smoothly.

During this testing phase, I simulate various user interactions and journey paths. For example, I might act as a new user signing up for the first time, or as an existing user browsing products and placing orders. I also test how the application handles errors and unexpected user inputs, which is crucial for providing a smooth user experience.

To extend my testing beyond my own interactions, I enlist the help of my friends and family. This provides fresh perspectives, as they may interact with the app in ways I hadn't anticipated. Furthermore, they can help me test the app on various devices and screen sizes to ensure the responsiveness and compatibility of the design across different platforms. This diversity in testing environments is invaluable, given the variety of devices users may use to access the app in real life.

Finally, once I've collated and addressed the feedback from these test users and am confident that the app functions as intended, it's time for the most thrilling step – launching the application! Deploying the app to the world is an exciting moment, seeing the product of my hard work and dedication finally accessible to the public.

9

Launch day

Launch day: it's a combination of excitement, anticipation, and a certain level of anxiety. It's the culmination of many late nights, iterations, and back-and-forth feedback sessions. Regardless of how you approach it, launch day is undoubtedly a significant milestone in the life of your startup.

Different businesses have different launch philosophies. Some prefer grand public rollouts with extensive PR campaigns. They see the launch as an opportunity to garner as much attention as possible to create a buzz that can give them a running start. This strategy certainly has its merits; an effective PR campaign can attract a significant initial user base, attract investors, and put your brand on the map.

However, a large-scale launch also comes with its own set of challenges. There's immense pressure to ensure that the product works flawlessly right off the bat, as any glitches can lead to negative publicity. Furthermore, with the intense media spotlight and high customer expectations, there's little room for error or adjustment.

On the other hand, some businesses opt for a more measured, quieter approach to their product launch. They might initially release their product to a select group of users, often loyal customers or early adopters who have been part of the product development journey. This approach enables the company to collect feedback and iron out any issues in a controlled environment before a broader rollout.

My personal preference leans towards this quieter, more calculated approach. From past experiences with startups, I've learned the value of a 'soft launch'. While it was exciting to see our product making headlines, the constant media attention became a distraction, shifting focus from product development to public relations. Moreover, the pressure of living up to the hype was intense. After all, putting your heart and soul into a project only to face the potential embarrassment of it malfunctioning on a public stage is no small feat. It's easy to get carried away with things like that. One of the tasks I've set for myself when building and testing new products is at the end of the day, I ask myself, 'How did I help my customers today?' It might have been simplifying my user experience or adding a new feature that they've been asking for. If I can answer that question at least once daily, I know I'm driving my product in the right direction.

Remember when we created a landing page so that we could collect the details of users who might be interesting in our product? Well, these are the people I invite to try my product first. They've already shown some interest by requesting further information, so their feedback is invaluable – it's often the case that they'll spot something you missed, whether it's a tiny glitch, a UI issue, or a simple spelling mistake.

What's most crucial here is the element of trust. You want these early users to provide honest feedback, but you also need them to be understanding and supportive as you navigate this crucial stage. With their help, you can continuously improve your product, preparing it for a broader audience.

Once you've refined the product based on your initial feedback, you can gradually expand your user base, bringing in those who have signed up for mailing lists or requested early access. This gradual approach allows you to control the narrative around your product, correct any issues that arise, and ensure that when your product does reach the masses, it's the best version of itself.

Ultimately, the path you choose for your launch day depends on your specific circumstances, your product, and your target audience. The key is to find the right balance between making a splash and ensuring your product is ready to face the world. After all, the purpose of a launch isn't just to celebrate the completion of a project but to embark on a new journey of growth, learning, and constant improvement.

When you do feel ready and you have ensured that your no-code startup's product or service is in a good state and ready for a broader audience (it doesn't need to be perfect – just usable), you can begin letting the world know about your launch. Here are some strategies you can use:

1. **Social media announcements:** It's essential to leverage all your social media channels, like Facebook, Instagram, Twitter, and LinkedIn, to create buzz around your launch. You could create a countdown to the launch date, behind-the-scenes sneak peeks, user testimonials, and even spotlight your team members working hard towards the launch. On the launch day, live updates, videos, or even a live stream could add to the excitement. Engage your audience by encouraging them to share your posts, leave comments, and interact with your content.

2. **Email blast:** An effective launch email is more than just announcing that your product is live. You can start by teasing the launch to your subscribers, drip-feeding information over time to create anticipation. Then, on launch day, send out a comprehensive email that explains the benefits of your product, perhaps including a demo video. Also, consider adding a limited-time offer to incentivize early adopters. Remember, personalization is key in emails, so address the receiver by their name and tailor your message based on what you know about them.

3. **Press releases:** A well-crafted press release can be a great way to get media coverage. It should be succinct, engaging, and include all the vital details about your product and the problem it solves. Including quotes from the founders and high-quality images can enhance the impact. After creating the press release, distribute it to journalists and bloggers who cover your industry, and consider using a PR distribution service to reach a wider audience.

4. **Influencer marketing:** Collaborating with influencers or thought leaders in your industry can lend credibility to your product and increase its visibility. It's crucial to find influencers whose audience aligns with your target customers. You could offer them early access to your product and ask for their honest reviews or collaborate on content such as sponsored posts, interviews, or webinars.

5. **Content marketing:** Sharing valuable, informative content can help position your startup as an expert in your industry. This could include blog posts, how-to guides, case studies, or explainer videos about your product. Consider SEO (Search Engine Optimization) strategies to help your content rank higher in search results, increasing your visibility.

6. **Paid advertising:** Paid ads on platforms like Google, Facebook, or LinkedIn can help you reach a wider audience. Carefully target your ads to reach your ideal customers based on demographics, interests, and online behaviour. Consider retargeting ads that follow users who have visited your website, reminding them of your product.

7. **Webinars or live streams:** Hosting a live event where you demonstrate your product in real-time can be a powerful way to engage potential users. During the event, answer questions, address concerns,

and showcase the unique features of your product. Consider inviting industry experts, influencers, or satisfied customers to join the event and share their insights or experiences.

8. **Network:** Leverage your existing network of personal contacts, professional colleagues, industry peers, and mentors. Share news of your launch through one-on-one interactions, at industry events, or via online communities and forums. Never underestimate the power of word-of-mouth recommendations.

9. **Customer testimonials:** Real-world reviews from satisfied customers can be a powerful endorsement of your product. Share these testimonials on your website, social media, and in your email blasts. Positive reviews help build trust with potential users.

10. **Launch on a product discovery platform:** Platforms like Product Hunt or BetaList are communities of tech enthusiasts who love discovering new products. Launching on these platforms can boost your visibility and attract an audience who are early adopters of new technology. Be ready to engage with the community, answer questions, and take on board feedback.

Remember that the more user you have, the more likely you will have to spend more on no-code subscriptions or API credits. If your startup is generating revenue straight away then you should be ok to cover those costs. If you're releasing an initial free product, those costs can stack up quickly, so be aware of this when you're inviting people to join.

Extra tech you may need

As a no-code startup founder, you'll quickly discover that even in the world of no-code, there are still some technical aspects to consider. Don't let this intimidate you. In this section, we'll cover the essential tech resources you may need, including domain acquisition, DNS settings, tracking tools, web and email hosting, and more.

Domain acquisition

Every online venture begins with buying a domain name, and the address of your startup on the internet. This can be a daunting process, particularly when faced with the sea of options available and the pressure to secure a perfect .com domain.

However, it's important not to get overly stressed about securing a .com domain. While .com is the most recognized and preferred extension, there are numerous other options like .io, .co, .net, .org, and even more specific ones like .tech or .ai. These can be just as effective, especially if they fit your business model or target audience better.

In addition, you also need to ensure that your chosen name doesn't infringe on any trademarks. Let me share a little story from my own experience. I once named my startup, let's call it 'X-Tool', only to receive a cease-and-desist letter from a company with a strikingly similar name that had trademarked it. This led to an abrupt and costly rebranding exercise. So, before you buy a domain, make sure to check for potential trademark conflicts to avoid such pitfalls.

DNS settings

Once you've secured your domain, you need to set up the Domain Name System (DNS) servers to point to your no-code product. Essentially, every website hosting provider or no-code website has a codename that identifies their whereabouts on the internet. You need to add that code or address to your domain name so that it knows where it needs to attach itself to.

Most domain registrars will provide instructions on how to change your DNS settings. Typically, it involves logging into your domain registrar account, finding the DNS settings page, and changing the DNS records to point to your no-code platform. For example, if you're using a platform like Bubble or Adalo, you would add a CNAME record with the values provided by these platforms.

Tracking tools

Tracking tools like Google Analytics and Facebook Pixel are essential for understanding your users' behaviour and optimizing your product.

Google Analytics 4, the latest version, offers a more integrated approach to data tracking and analysis. To install it, you first need to create a Google Analytics account and set up a 'property' for your website. You'll be provided with a tracking code which needs to be installed on every page of your website. Depending on your no-code tool, this might involve pasting the code into a specific input field or using a plugin.

Similarly, Facebook Pixel allows you to track conversions from Facebook ads, optimize ads, build targeted audiences, and re-engage with users. To install it, you need to create a pixel in your Facebook Events Manager, and then add the pixel code to your website.

Remember, these tools collect user data, so you need to ensure you're compliant with data protection regulations.

Web and email hosting

Web hosting is generally taken care of by your no-code platform. However, if you're self-hosting a tool like WordPress, you'll need to select a reliable web hosting provider. Look for providers that offer excellent uptime, customer support, and compatibility with WordPress.

Custom email addresses aren't technically vital when it comes to testing your business, but as a rule, I always get a custom email for any product I'm developing. First, I think it's much more professional to email potential customers with myname@mycompany.com than an email that ends in @gmail.com or @hotmail.com. There is nothing wrong with these emails of course, but I think if you're asking a stranger to trust you and give you money for a product or service then you should look the part. Second, it also helps the receiver to remember your company if they can see your startup name in the email address.

Providers like Google Workspace and Microsoft 365 offer custom email addresses along with productivity tools.

If you opt for this, you'll need to update your domain's MX (Mail Exchanger) records to point to your email host. The process typically involves logging into your domain registrar's control panel, navigating to your domain settings, and changing the MX records to those provided by your email host.

Here's a general step-by-step guide:

1. **Purchase an email hosting plan:** First, choose an email hosting provider and purchase an email hosting plan that suits your needs. You'll be provided with a set of MX records that point to the email servers of your email hosting provider. These records will look something like this: ASPMX.L.GOOGLE.COM.

2. **Log in to your domain registrar account:** This is where you purchased your domain. Common registrars include GoDaddy, Namecheap, or Bluehost.

3. **Navigate to the DNS settings:** Look for a section labelled 'DNS Settings', 'Domain Settings', or something similar. Here, you'll see a list of all the current DNS records for your domain.

4. **Update the MX records:** You'll need to replace the existing MX records with the new ones provided by your email hosting provider. There may be multiple records, and it's important to enter them exactly as provided. MX records typically come with a priority

number that dictates the order in which they should be tried. Lower numbers have higher priority.

5. **Save your changes:** Make sure to save your changes before exiting the control panel.

6. **Wait for propagation:** It can take anywhere from a few minutes to 48 hours for these changes to propagate across the internet. During this time, you may not be able to receive emails at your new domain-based email addresses.

Remember, each domain registrar may have slightly different interfaces and processes, so it's always best to consult their specific documentation or support if you're unsure.

10

Getting the basics of your startup right

Building and launching your app is only a small aspect of creating a successful startup. There are so many other elements that you need to manage daily if you have any hope of surviving and growing. Thankfully, no-code can help you in ways that Steve Jobs and Bill Gates could only dream of!

Managing the money

Navigating the financial maze of a startup can be quite a challenge, especially when every decision you make could either make or break your venture. For a no-code founder, managing money becomes even more significant due to the variable costs of no-code subscriptions, API tokens, domains, marketing, and other operational expenses. Despite the relative affordability of no-code tools, costs can pile up quickly. In this section, we'll delve into the art of bootstrapping and explore how no-code founders can effectively manage their finances to test their ideas and grow their startups.

Bootstrapping: The self-funding way

Bootstrapping is a funding approach where entrepreneurs establish and scale their startups using personal savings or initial business revenue. It's a path of self-reliance that encourages lean operations with an emphasis on profitability from the get-go. This strategy allows founders to retain full control and ownership of their companies, free from investor intervention or equity dilution.

Let's take a closer look at the benefits and potential challenges of bootstrapping.

Benefits of bootstrapping

The benefits of bootstrapping are compelling. The first and foremost advantage is full control over the company. As a founder, you have the freedom to steer your startup in any direction you deem fit without needing to satisfy external investors' demands.

Bootstrapping also allows for a greater equity share, which means if your startup becomes profitable, you reap a larger portion of the benefits. The decision-making process becomes quicker and more efficient without the need for consensus from multiple stakeholders.

This approach compels founders to focus on generating revenue early. Without the cushion of external funds, you're driven to create a sustainable and profitable business model. It also frees you from the pressure of investor expectations, allowing you to focus on building a product that truly resonates with your target customers.

The bootstrap path for no-code founders

As a no-code founder, you have an added advantage when bootstrapping. The emergence of various no-code tools has made it possible to build fully functional apps and platforms without heavy investments. Tools like Bubble, Adalo, and Zapier replace the need for expensive developers, thereby significantly reducing startup costs.

You can start building your product using these tools with a minimal upfront investment. As your user base grows, your subscription costs might increase, but ideally, so would your revenue. If you're offering your product for free, it's crucial to devise a monetization strategy that could sustain your growing costs. This could involve advertising, partnerships, premium features, or future fundraising when your product has gained traction.

Real-life bootstrapping: A personal account

In my previous startup, I was fortunate to secure a place on a tech accelerator that gave us a £10,000 grant to use over a six-month period. We were lucky to have this, as many founders start out with only their own personal savings. Either way, boot-strapping means learning how to make every last penny stretch as far as it can. With just two of us in the team, we knew we had to be frugal. For an entire year, this amount covered our essential business expenses. To supplement our personal needs, we took on freelance work in the evenings.

With my current venture, Willo.social, I started on a tighter budget of £200. I took care of ongoing costs through my private income, again highlighting the possibilities of bootstrapping. The experience of managing a lean budget, prioritizing business essentials, and supplementing income through freelancing served as practical lessons in financial discipline and resilience.

Alternatives to bootstrapping: Pros and cons

Bootstrapping isn't the only way to fund a startup. Alternatives like venture capital, angel investment, and crowdfunding can offer a significant capital boost. However, these options come with their downsides.

External funding can accelerate your growth, but it often leads to loss of control and equity dilution. Investors expect high growth rates and a solid exit strategy, which could shift the focus from building a sustainable business to meeting investor expectations. Such pressure may result in a deviation from your original vision or even lead to hasty decisions that might not be in the best interest of the startup in the long run.

On the other hand, having an external investor can bring in much-needed expertise, industry connections, and credibility. Their involvement can potentially accelerate the growth trajectory and increase the chances of success. However, it's crucial to carefully consider these trade-offs and align your funding decisions with your startup's long-term objectives and your personal comfort with risk and control.

Money management tips for no-code founders

As a no-code founder, managing your finances wisely is crucial for sustainable growth. Here are some tips based on my personal experiences:

1. **Lean operations:** Operate with minimal costs. Use cost-effective no-code tools to build your product. Instead of hiring a full-time team, consider freelancing or outsourcing for non-core activities.

2. **Prioritize spending:** Only spend on essentials that contribute to your business growth. For instance, rather than splurging on a fancy office, consider a co-working space or working from home.

3. **Monetize early:** If you plan to offer your product for free initially, consider how you can monetize it. This could be through in-app purchases, premium features, advertising, partnerships, or even a freemium model where basic services are free, but advanced features come at a cost.

4. **Supplement your income:** If possible, consider taking up freelance work or consulting in your area of expertise. This can help cover personal expenses and even some business costs.

5. **Track and monitor expenses:** Regularly review your expenses and trim any unnecessary spending. Use budgeting tools or software to keep a close eye on your cash flow.

6. **Have a financial buffer:** Bootstrapping can be risky. If your product takes longer to generate revenue, you need a buffer to keep your startup afloat. Ensure you have some personal savings or a fallback plan.

7. **Fundraising:** Once your product has gained some traction, you may consider fundraising as a way to fuel growth. However, ensure that you're ready for the responsibilities and expectations that come with external funding.

Bootstrapping as a no-code founder is a challenging but rewarding journey. It compels you to prioritize, operate lean, and focus on profitability. While it comes with its share of risks, the reward is retaining full control of your company and the satisfaction of building a business from the ground up. Despite the financial constraints, remember that many successful startups, including MailChimp, GitHub, and Basecamp, started their journeys with bootstrapping. With careful planning, disciplined spending, and a bit of creativity, you can successfully bootstrap your no-code startup.

Where to find startup credits for supporting software

As well as your no-code tools, you may need to buy into additional software to help manage your business, such as server space (if you want to host things like video) or document storage.

Luckily many large companies offer free credits or reduced subscription costs for startups. You'll likely have to apply for some of these programs but once you are in, the benefits can be invaluable. Some of these tools can be used as a no-code tool in itself, whilst others can provide additional features that may help you.

AWS (Amazon Web Services), to a non-techie, is a daunting and complex suite of tools. However, it can still be beneficial to a no-code founder. AWS provides a range of services that go beyond traditional coding and can be used with a variety of no-code or low-code platforms. Here are some of the ways you can leverage AWS as a no-code founder:

1. **AWS Honeycode:** This is a fully managed service that allows you to quickly build mobile and web applications with no programming required. You can create applications using a simple visual interface, and Honeycode will handle the rest, including the backend, storage, computing, and security.

2. **Amazon S3:** This is a storage service that can be used to store and retrieve any amount of data at any time. It can be used in conjunction with a variety of no-code platforms to manage and store user data, images, videos, and other content.

3. **Amazon Cognito:** This service provides user sign-up, sign-in, and access control to web and mobile apps without requiring any backend code. It can be integrated with many no-code platforms to handle user authentication and authorization.

4. **AWS Amplify:** While it's more of a low-code solution, Amplify provides a set of tools and services that enable mobile and front-end web developers to build secure, scalable full-stack applications. It can be beneficial if you're using a low-code platform that allows for some customization and coding.

5. **API Gateway:** This lets you create, publish, maintain, monitor, and secure APIs at any scale. This is useful if your no-code solution needs to interact with other services and you need a secure and scalable way to manage these interactions.

6. **Various database options:** AWS offers managed database services like Amazon DynamoDB (NoSQL) and Amazon RDS (relational databases like MySQL, PostgreSQL etc.). These can be used as the backend for your no-code applications.

7. **AWS Activate:** AWS Activate is a bespoke program specifically designed to cater to the needs of startups, offering a myriad of invaluable resources to jumpstart their initiatives on Amazon Web Services. The program serves up much more than cloud services; it offers a bounty of credits, thorough training, and robust support to help startups create, launch, and expand their ideas on AWS.

The IBM Cloud offers a variety of services that can be utilized by non-technical founders and used in conjunction with no-code platforms. Here's how IBM Cloud can be beneficial:

1. **IBM Cloudant:** IBM Cloudant is a fully managed JSON document database that's optimized for data availability, durability, and mobility. It's perfect for web and mobile apps, and its API is compatible with applications created using no-code platforms.

2. **IBM Watson Services:** The Watson suite offers a range of AI services that can be accessed via APIs, making them usable with no-code platforms. This includes Watson Assistant for building conversational interfaces, Watson Discovery for insights from data, and more.

3. **IBM App Connect:** This allows you to automate workflows and integrate data, apps, and APIs across your environment. It's a kind of no-code tool itself, enabling you to connect different applications and services without writing any code.

4. **Cloud Functions:** IBM's serverless platform can run code in response to events, such as changes to data in a database or user actions in a mobile app. This is more of a low-code solution but can be beneficial if your no-code platform allows for some custom coding.

5. **Databases:** IBM Cloud offers a selection of databases like IBM Db2 (relational database), IBM Cloud Databases for PostgreSQL, etc. These can be used as a backend for your no-code applications.

6. **API Management:** IBM's API Connect lets you create, manage, secure and socialize your APIs across hybrid cloud environments. This is useful for no-code applications that need to interact with other services.

In general, the value of the IBM Cloud for a no-code founder comes from its wide array of managed services, many of which can be integrated with no-code tools.

Startup with IBM: Striving to act as a revolutionary force for startups, Startup with IBM offers an impressive $120,000 in IBM Cloud credits. The objective of this program is to disrupt industries by arming startups with top-tier cloud technology, thereby setting them on a course towards notable growth.

Google Cloud: Google offers a variety of services that can be utilized even if you are not writing code yourself. Here's how Google Cloud can be beneficial:

1. **Firebase:** Firebase is a development platform for app developers that provides a variety of tools and services to help you develop high-quality apps, grow your user base, and earn more money. Firebase includes services for analytics, hosting, authentication, real-time databases, and more. Most of these services are accessible via APIs and SDKs, making them usable with many no-code platforms.

2. **Google Cloud Storage:** This is an object storage service for any amount of data at any time. It is typically used for archiving, backup and recovery, content distribution, and data analysis. This could be used in conjunction with a no-code platform to store and serve data.

3. **Google Cloud's machine learning and AI services:** Google Cloud offers a variety of machine learning and AI services, like Vision AI for image analysis, Natural Language API for text analysis, and Recommendations AI for personalized recommendations. These can be accessed via APIs, making them usable with no-code platforms.

4. **Google Workspace:** This suite of cloud computing, productivity, and collaboration tools, software, and products can be integrated with many no-code platforms to build productivity apps.

5. **Google Maps Platform:** This service offers SDKs and APIs to add maps, routes, and places to your no-code applications.

6. **Google Cloud's serverless computing solutions like Cloud Functions and Cloud Run:** These can be used to execute code without managing servers. This is more of a low-code solution, but it can be beneficial if your no-code platform allows for some custom coding.

7. **BigQuery:** Google's fully managed and scalable data warehouse can be used for analytics. While it requires SQL to query the data, there are no-code platforms that support SQL.

Google Cloud for Startups: This program propels startups to break new ground with resources such as mentorship, training, and Cloud credits. Google Cloud for Startups aims to cultivate swift and efficient development by equipping startups with a powerful infrastructure to build their projects.

Microsoft: Many of Microsoft's tools and services can be effectively utilized in a no-code context. Here's how:

1. **Microsoft Azure:** Azure is Microsoft's cloud platform, offering over 200 products and cloud services. While

many of these are more developer-oriented, there are several that can be useful in a no-code context:

2. **Azure Logic Apps:** This is a cloud service that helps you schedule, automate, and orchestrate tasks, business processes, and workflows when you need to integrate apps, data, systems, and services across enterprises or organizations.

3. **Power Automate:** Formerly known as Microsoft Flow, this service allows you to automate repetitive tasks by creating workflows between your favourite apps and services.

4. **Microsoft 365:** This suite of productivity tools includes familiar software like Word, Excel, and PowerPoint, as well as collaboration tools like Teams and SharePoint. Many no-code platforms can integrate with these tools to provide enhanced functionality.

5. **Power Apps:** This is a suite of apps, services, connectors, and data platforms that provides a rapid application development environment to build custom apps for your business needs. Using Power Apps, you can quickly build custom business apps that connect to your business data stored either in the underlying data platform (Microsoft Dataverse) or in various online and on-premises data sources (SharePoint, Microsoft 365, Dynamics 365, SQL Server, and so on).

6. **Power BI:** This is a business analytics tool that lets you visualize your data and share insights across your organization. It can be used to connect to hundreds of data sources, simplify data prep, and drive ad hoc analysis.

7. **GitHub:** Microsoft's GitHub platform can be used for version control, even in a no-code context. For

example, you can use GitHub to manage and version control your no-code website's source files.

8. **Azure DevOps:** This is a set of development tools for planning, developing, testing, and delivering software. While mostly targeted at code-based development, some features like project planning and tracking can be beneficial for no-code projects as well.

Microsoft for Startups: With a significant commitment of 500 million dollars over the forthcoming two years, Microsoft for Startups aims to nurture innovation and expansion in the startup community. The program extends access to state-of-the-art technology, cooperative community spaces, and sales opportunities to help startups flourish.

Twilio Segment: Recognizing the importance of customer data for startups in their quest for product-market fit, Twilio Segment offers its services free for up to two years to early-stage startups. The program aids them in collecting and analyzing vital customer data while providing additional benefits.

HubSpot for Startups: HubSpot proffers a comprehensive array of tools engineered to propel startup growth. Their CRM, sales, marketing, and customer service software, supplemented with educational resources and dedicated support, assist startups in cultivating robust relationships with customers and scaling effectively.

Intercom for Early Stage: Intercom offers an array of intuitive products designed to assist startups in engaging with their customers on a more personal level. Eligible startups gain access to all of Intercom's pro products at a fixed rate of $49 per month for up to one year.

Startup accelerators are another way of getting not only an abundance of free credits but also a way to learn how to build a successful startup. Accelerators are specially designed programs that offer startups mentorship, resources, and sometimes even capital, usually in exchange for a small equity stake. They typically conclude with a demo day, where startups present their progress and future plans to an audience filled with potential investors. Accelerators can be a potent method to rapidly accelerate growth and refine a business idea. They often provide a structured environment that aids founders in sidestepping common startup missteps while also offering a network of mentors and alumni who can provide invaluable advice and connections. I'll talk a little more about my experience with accelerators in Chapter twelve.

11

Grow or pivot

This chapter holds significant value for your business journey. By now, you might have developed a product that customers appreciate, use regularly, and are even willing to pay for. But the challenge lies in identifying and tracking those crucial metrics that validate your product's success to both you and external parties, such as potential customers and investors. Which metrics truly matter? Is it the number of product downloads, the views on our app, or perhaps our follower count on social media? And if these metrics indicate a lack of interest, does that signal the end or a need for a pivot?

Every business is unique, and so are the answers to these questions. Let's delve into the process of selecting the most relevant metrics, gathering them, and then leveraging this data to make informed decisions about your product's trajectory.

Collecting data to inform your decisions

Customer interviews

One of the most effective ways to understand your user experience is by conducting customer interviews. Direct, one-on-one interaction with users can provide you with deep, qualitative insights that you can't obtain from data analysis alone. During these interviews, you can ask open-ended questions that allow users to express their thoughts, feelings, and ideas about your product freely.

To conduct efficient customer interviews, prepare a list of targeted questions beforehand. For example, you might want to ask about the user's overall experience, any difficulties they encountered, features they found useful, and any improvements they'd like to see. Remember, the goal is not to sell but to listen and learn.

Recording user interactions

An essential tool in your feedback arsenal is a screen recording tool. By recording user interactions with your product, you can observe firsthand how they navigate your interface, how long they engage with certain features, and where they encounter difficulties.

This was a technique I used in the early stages of my startup, Willo.Social. I recorded every user session and noted their interactions with the platform. I didn't rely on my memory but instead revisited these recordings to document all the points they raised. This approach provided a clear, unbiased view of the user experience, which was critical in shaping the development of Willo.Social.

Surveys and analytical tools

Surveys can provide you with a broader, quantitative perspective on user feedback. Use survey tools to ask questions about their experience and to gauge their satisfaction levels. You can also use these tools to collect demographic information that may provide additional context to their feedback.

Complement surveys with analytical tools. These can help you understand user behaviour on your platform. Metrics such as session duration, bounce rate, and conversion rate can provide insights into user engagement and satisfaction.

Understanding the value of payment and cancellations

Two of the most significant indicators of your product's value are whether users are willing to pay for it and whether they decide to cancel their subscription. A user willing to pay for your product is a strong signal that your product is delivering value. On the other hand, if users are cancelling their subscriptions, it's crucial to understand why.

With Willo.Social, I made a point of reaching out to users who decided to cancel their subscriptions. Their feedback often provided the most valuable insights. They helped me understand which areas needed improvement and often gave insights into features or aspects I hadn't considered.

Making sense of data you've collected

Documenting feedback

Every piece of feedback, whether positive, negative, or suggesting new features, is valuable. It's crucial to document all the feedback you receive systematically. Use a feedback management tool or even a simple spreadsheet to help organize and categorize feedback. This will allow you to identify patterns and recurring themes, providing a more holistic understanding of user experiences and needs.

Understanding and embracing user feedback is an integral part of running a successful startup. As your no-code business begins to gain traction, dedicate time and resources to collecting insights from your users, analyzing this data, and implementing changes based on this feedback.

User feedback helps you gauge your product's effectiveness, identify shortcomings, and uncover opportunities for improvement. It provides you with the direct voice of your customer – a tool of immeasurable value for enhancing your product and user experience.

Remember that every piece of feedback, whether it's a complaint, a compliment, or a suggestion for a new feature, provides an opportunity to learn and improve. As I experienced with Willo.Social, some of the most valuable insights can come from unexpected places.

Always remember that customer feedback is not about affirmation. It's about understanding, learning, and growth. The more feedback you gather and act upon, the more your no-code startup will be primed for success. It's also easy to get carried away with both good and bad data. I had been so excited when a handful of users were highly complementary of what I had created, that I felt like I had conquered Everest and had no need to keep going with my validation. On the opposite end of the spectrum, I've had times when people didn't like what I'd built and I really took it to heart. In either scenario, you almost have to try and remain impartial and objective.

The unexpected insights

In gathering user feedback for Willo.Social, one recurring theme was users' desire to connect virtually with others. I built the app with a focus on fostering local, physical meetups. However, I quickly learned that many users also wanted the option of virtual meetups for days they couldn't leave the house.

Additionally, users expressed a desire to connect with local venues as much as with other people. This feedback was unexpected and something I hadn't initially considered. But it emphasized the importance of gathering user feedback: users can provide insights and ideas that you, as the founder, might not think of.

Pivoting your idea

When you're analyzing your data, there may be point (or several points) where everything is telling you that something is not working. Maybe the features you have created are not really helping your customers, or maybe they're only using one tiny bit of your product and not the part you thought they might. This is really where making sense of your data really is important because it could save you from hours of wasted time, energy, and money.

If your data is telling you that have a problem, it may be that you need to pivot your product or your idea entirely. In the startup universe, 'pivoting' refers to a strategic shift that steers a startup in a new direction in response to market feedback or real-time insights. Pivoting, often perceived as an act of desperation or failure, is actually a course correction designed to test a new approach for the fulfilment of a startup's vision. It's an acknowledgement of an idea that may not be working and a shift towards a potentially more profitable and efficient direction. As a no-code founder, you have the advantage of making this shift seamlessly with minimal time and financial loss.

Understanding your customer data is vital to ascertain whether a pivot is needed. It could be an aspect of your app that's not resonating with users, or it could be the whole concept. User feedback, product usage metrics, and interaction patterns can provide valuable insights into what works and what doesn't. If multiple users express a similar desire for a different feature or functionality, that could be your cue to pivot.

Notably, some of today's most successful startups owe their victories to well-timed pivots. Below, I have listed a few inspiring examples.

PayPal: Rooted in the realm of payments

PayPal's journey is a testament to multiple strategic shifts. Its precursor, Confinity, created in 1999, was designed to facilitate 'beam' payments via Personal Digital Assistants (PDAs). The merging with X.com redirected its focus towards becoming a dominant online payment service, fuelled by the burgeoning growth of eBay. Thus, PayPal, with its flexible approach, evolved to be a household name in online payment processing.

Flickr: From a game to photo-sharing phenomenon

What started as an online role-playing game, 'Game Neverending', quickly identified the rising popularity of its photo-sharing feature amongst users. The company leveraged this user behaviour, pivoted, and gave birth to Flickr. Yahoo's acquisition of Flickr in 2005 marked one of the most successful pivots in the digital industry.

Pinterest: A pivot towards collective creativity

Originally known as 'Tote', Pinterest was a platform that allowed users to shop from their favourite retailers and get updates on sales. As users exhibited an affinity for creating 'collections' of favourite items and sharing them, the company identified an opportunity. A pivot towards this 'collecting and sharing' model resulted in Pinterest, a platform that boasts over 70 million users today.

X: Microblogging success born out of a podcast network

The transformation from Odeo, a podcast subscription network, to X, a status-updating microblogging platform, is one of the most celebrated pivots in social media history. With iTunes emerging as a major player in the podcasting niche, Odeo anticipated its obsolescence. A shift towards the idea of a micro-blogging platform by Jack Dorsey and Biz Stone positioned X as a global leader in social media.

Netflix: A master of evolution

Netflix's evolution is a perfect illustration of strategic pivots driven by technological progression and user behaviour. Starting as a mail-order DVD service, Netflix anticipated the shift towards digital consumption and introduced downloadable and streaming content. Predicting a future where studios could stream content directly to consumers, Netflix again pivoted and began creating its original content. Its foresight and readiness to evolve allowed it to stay relevant and competitive in a fast-paced industry.

Pivoting, though sounds daunting, is a tactical manoeuvre to align with evolving market trends and consumer expectations. It is less about abandoning an initial idea and more about refining it to create value for your users and build a sustainable business. Remember, the key to a successful pivot lies in understanding your customer feedback and using it to redefine your product or service strategically. As a no-code founder, this agility to pivot comes as a boon, helping you reshape your product seamlessly, quickly, and cost-effectively.

With the advent of no-code platforms, the ability to pivot has become more accessible than ever before. The traditional process of rewriting code, deploying new versions, and the associated expenses have been replaced with much more flexible processes. Today, you can experiment, test, and iterate rapidly without any substantial sunk costs. No-code platforms allow you to build your applications as a series of modular, customizable blocks that can be rearranged and reconfigured as needed.

But, it's essential to remember that while pivoting offers a pathway towards a new opportunity, it also requires a clear understanding of why the previous path did not work. It's not a decision to be taken lightly or frequently, but rather a calculated move based on detailed analysis and insights. The last thing you want is to end up in an endless pivot cycle, where you continually chase new ideas without fully understanding or addressing the issues that led to the need for a pivot in the first place.

I recently met a founder who had built a vetted student dating app in no-code. He did everything right; he spoke to potential customers, identified the problem, etc. Just as he launched, a major brand released an identical product in the space. Because they already had market dominance, he decided to go back to his users and re-evaluate the problems they were facing. His dating app became a study group app where students could meet locally and virtually for study and group discussion. A simple pivot ended up being the winning idea that resonated with many students.

Whether it's PayPal which transitioned from 'beaming' payments to becoming a dominant online payment service, or X which emerged from a podcast network, successful pivots demonstrate the importance of staying flexible, listening to customer feedback, and being ready to reinvent yourself. Your initial idea might offer a starting point, but it's your ability to learn, adapt, and pivot that will ultimately determine your success in the startup world. As Reid Hoffman, co-founder of LinkedIn, once said, 'An entrepreneur is someone who will jump off a cliff and assemble an aeroplane on the way down'. With no-code platforms and the ability to pivot, you're essentially given the tools to build and modify your aeroplane mid-flight based on the winds of customer feedback and market trends.

Choosing to pivot

Prototyping 2.0

So, what happens after you decide to pivot, either completely or partially? Well, we now use our even greater insight to build version 2.0. The first time you built your prototype, you were likely learning how to use your no-code tool and figuring out the best way to bring your idea to life. But now, having navigated through the complexities of your first build, you are equipped with a wealth of experience that can streamline your second build process. You're familiar with the no-code tool you've been using, you understand its strengths, and you know how to work around its limitations. This expertise allows you to build more efficiently and confidently, resulting in a more polished and refined product.

In the unpredictable realm of startup entrepreneurship, the stage of constructing your second prototype – referred to as 'Prototyping 2.0' in this discussion – emerges as a pivotal juncture. At this transformative milestone, your entrepreneurial venture embarks on an evolutionary path, internalizing insights from past experiences and using them as catalysts for growth and improvement. This endeavour is not one-size-fits-all; rather, it is as varied as the startup ecosystem itself. It could demand a comprehensive overhaul of your product, a series of nuanced adaptations, or just a minor course correction. Regardless of the scope, it is not solely a technical exercise. It is a strategic venture firmly grounded in user feedback, comprehension of market dynamics, and the unique value proposition of your business.

A question that often lingers in the minds of startup founders at this stage is whether to rebuild the product from scratch or to repurpose the existing prototype. The answer hinges primarily on the nature and extent of changes that your product requires.

If your business model has undergone a radical transformation or if your initial prototype was primarily an exploratory endeavour, embarking on a fresh start might be a more viable strategy. Conversely, if your pivot entails modifying or adding certain features, then adjusting your existing prototype could provide a more resource-efficient solution.

A comparative examination of my experience with Willo. Social and the journey of a dating app founder illuminates this point. When the need arose to incorporate new features into Willo.Social, I decided to create a fresh version using the Bubble platform. The initial platform was useful during the early stages, but the requirement for added features and scalability factors necessitated a fresh start. Contrarily, the dating app founder experienced a shift in his business direction. However, the fundamental architecture of connecting people by interest and location still held relevance. Consequently, he capitalized on 80% of his original Bubble build and refined the remaining aspects to align with the new business trajectory.

Capitalizing on no-code flexibility in Prototyping 2.0

No-code platforms bring a unique quality to the table – their exceptional adaptability and flexibility. They enable rapid prototyping without exerting undue demands on critical resources – time and finances. Whether the transition demands a comprehensive overhaul, modification of existing features, or the introduction of new ones, no-code tools facilitate an efficient and streamlined shift.

A complete rebuild, while it may seem intimidating, is not as daunting in the realm of no-code tools as it would be with traditional coding methods. Armed with the experience and insights gained during the creation of your initial prototype, the construction of the second version is often a more streamlined, efficient, and well-planned process.

Building a second prototype without a pivot

Interestingly, the impetus for Prototyping 2.0 does not always stem from the necessity to pivot or make significant adjustments. Some founders, having achieved proficiency in the no-code tool they have been using, elect to build a second version of their app simply to leverage their enhanced understanding of the tool. Recognizing the value of a more efficient, 'cleaner' version of their app, they undertake a rebuild even without implementing any substantial changes to the product or its features.

Choosing to grow

When your metrics indicate that customers are enjoying and actively using your product, take a moment to acknowledge your accomplishment. Achieving this level of success is commendable and deserves recognition. But remember, the journey doesn't end here. It's essential to maintain momentum. Now, you must contemplate the future: How will you scale your product? How can you enhance its value for users? And importantly, what's your timeline for these next steps?

Creating a product roadmap for new features

Once you are happy that your fundamental product is robust, functional, and satisfying your customers' needs, it's time to start looking at making your product even better with new features. This milestone can arrive at any iteration – be it your first, second, or even third prototype. At this juncture, it becomes imperative to map out the future of your product.

This roadmap, aptly called a product roadmap, is where you set the direction for your product's evolution. While the actual path might change over time due to market trends, user feedback, or technological advancements, having a plan enables you to make informed decisions and provides your team with a sense of direction and purpose. In this section, we will delve into the creation of a product roadmap, specifically focusing on prioritizing features based on user feedback.

Creating a feature suggestion mechanism

Before you can prioritize features, you need a systematic way of capturing suggestions. A simple and effective method is to include a 'suggest a feature' form on your website. This form can be embedded directly into your site using a tool like Typeform. By linking this form to Google Sheets, you can automate the process of collecting suggestions, making the data immediately available for analysis and decision-making. This streamlines the process and ensures that none of the valuable insights from your users are lost.

Working with user feedback

Over time, as your user base grows and more people engage with your product, you'll accumulate a wealth of suggestions. This user feedback is an invaluable resource – it gives you direct insight into what your users want, what problems they're facing, and what enhancements could make their experience better. However, it's critical to remember that not all suggestions can, or should, be implemented. Just like with your MVP, you need to prioritize features based on their potential impact on your product and their alignment with your business goals.

Return to MoSCoW method for prioritizing feedback

To help you in this prioritization process, you can return to the MoSCoW method that you used when first defining your MVP. The categories of 'must have', 'should have', 'could have', and 'won't have' can be applied to your list of suggested features as well. The 'must have' features are those that are essential for your product's functionality or that address a significant user need. The 'should have' features, while important, are not as critical. The 'could have' features are desirable but not necessary, and the 'won't have' features are those that you decide not to implement at this stage.

Building a product roadmap

Once we have finished working through our user feedback, we need to start thinking about our plans for how we're going to keeping moving our product forward. We do this by creating something called a product roadmap.

A product roadmap is a visual representation of your product's evolution. It outlines the planned changes, enhancements, and additions to your product over time. More specifically, it provides an overview of what features you plan to develop when you plan to release them, and why they're important. This 'why' should be grounded in your understanding of your users, your product, and your market.

Your product roadmap should begin with a clear statement of your product's vision and objectives. This provides a guiding light for all your decisions and ensures that your roadmap aligns with your business goals. Following this, you can list the features you plan to develop, categorized using the MoSCoW method.

For each feature, you should provide a brief description, an estimate of its impact on your product, and a timeline for its development and release. This timeline can be flexible – its purpose is to provide a rough idea of when each feature will be available, not to set rigid deadlines.

Finally, it's important to remember that a product roadmap is a dynamic document – it should evolve as your product does. As you receive more user feedback, as market trends change, or as new opportunities arise, you should revisit your roadmap and adjust it as necessary.

The art of prioritization

One of the trickiest elements of growing our product, is knowing what to build next and when. If you're like me, the excitement of seeing your hard work coming to fruition is sometimes hard to resist and you can end up building something your customers don't quite need yet.

Prioritization is a vital part of the product development process. In a perfect world, we would have unlimited resources to implement every feature our users suggest. However, in reality, we must carefully choose which features will bring the most value to our customers and align with our business goals.

This is where your product roadmap comes into play. It provides a clear, visual representation of your priorities, helping you make informed decisions about what to focus on. One strategy for prioritization is to evaluate each proposed feature based on two main factors: user value and business value.

User value represents the importance of a feature to your users. This can be determined through user feedback, surveys, or user testing. Business value, on the other hand, refers to the impact a feature will have on your business, such as increasing revenue, reducing costs, or improving operational efficiency.

By evaluating each feature based on these factors, you can identify which ones will bring the most value to both your users and your business. These should be your top priorities.

Also, consider the effort required to implement each feature. A feature that brings high value but requires minimal effort would be a higher priority than one that brings similar value but requires more resources. This is often referred to as a cost-benefit analysis.

Implementing the roadmap

Once you have your roadmap and have prioritized your features, it's time to put it into action. This will typically involve several steps, including design, development, testing, and release.

Remember that the goal is not to rush through this process but to ensure that each feature is implemented effectively and delivers the intended value. It's also essential to gather user feedback after each release to understand if the feature is meeting user needs and how it can be improved.

Iterating on the roadmap

Your product roadmap is not set in stone. As you gather more feedback, you may find that some features are more important than you initially thought, while others are less impactful. You may also discover new features that you hadn't considered before.

Therefore, it's crucial to continually revisit your roadmap, updating it based on the latest feedback, insights, and business objectives. This iterative process ensures that your product continues to evolve in a way that meets user needs and contributes to your business's success.

Embracing a culture of continuous improvement

A critical aspect of managing a product roadmap is fostering a culture of continuous improvement. Each new feature should be viewed as an opportunity to learn and improve. Whether a feature is a hit with users or falls flat, there is always something to be learned that can inform future decisions.

Even after a feature is launched, the job is not complete. Regularly check in on how each feature is performing and how users are responding to it. Use these insights to make adjustments and continue improving your product over time.

Creating a product roadmap and prioritizing features is a crucial part of developing a successful product. By systematically gathering user feedback, evaluating features based on user and business value, and continuously iterating on your roadmap, you can ensure that your product continues to evolve in a way that delights your users and drives your business forward. This iterative, data-driven approach to product development is at the heart of the no-code methodology, enabling startups to quickly adapt to user needs and market trends.

A guide to metrics: Measuring the right data

Selecting the right data to inform your product roadmap

In the business world, data and metrics are paramount. They are the compass that points your business in the right direction, the anchor that grounds your decision-making process in reality, and the engine that propels your startup's growth. However, not all data is created equal, and as a founder, it's crucial to distinguish between 'vanity metrics' and 'actionable metrics'. Understanding the difference, and knowing how to leverage the right metrics, is pivotal for the long-term success of your startup.

Vanity metrics vs. actionable metrics: A tale of two data points

Let's delve into what each type of metric represents. Vanity metrics are data points that might initially seem impressive but don't necessarily contribute to your business's core growth or profitability. They are termed 'vanity' metrics because they often serve to inflate the ego rather than inform your strategy. This category includes metrics such as the number of app downloads, website hits, social media followers, press features, and awards won.

Take, for example, an Instagram influencer boasting about having 10,000 followers. On the surface, this metric paints a picture of success and popularity, making it appealing to advertisers. However, if you drill down further, it could reveal that only a few hundred followers actively engage with their posts. This implies that the majority of followers may not be genuinely interested in the influencer's content and, therefore, an advertiser would derive little value from collaborating with them.

Actionable metrics, on the other hand, offer meaningful insights that can directly inform business decisions and actions. These are the numbers that genuinely reflect the health and growth trajectory of your startup. They include metrics such as customer acquisition cost (CAC), customer lifetime value (CLTV), churn rate (the percentage of customers who stop using your product over a specific period), retention rate (the percentage of customers who continue to use your product over a specific period), conversion rate, and revenue growth.

What metrics should matter to your business?

The specific metrics you should focus on will hinge upon your unique business model and the current stage of your startup. For instance, in their early days, B2C startups like Facebook concentrated primarily on user growth, even before they had a clear revenue model. This was because their value proposition was rooted in network effects: the more people who used Facebook, the more valuable it became for each user. This model appealed to investors who saw the massive potential once monetization strategies were deployed at scale.

Conversely, B2B startups may need to demonstrate a steady revenue stream and a solid base of paying customers from early on to draw investor interest. In a B2B model, where sales cycles are often longer and customer acquisition costs are higher, revenue and customer retention are key indicators of sustainable growth.

Monitoring key metrics: A hands-on approach

You can maintain a simple yet effective method of tracking key metrics by using a spreadsheet. Columns can be dedicated to metrics such as customer sign-ups, customer conversions, churn rate, advertising spend per conversion, and more, updating it at regular intervals.

Harnessing no-code tools for data tracking

In today's digital landscape, no-code tools have revolutionized the way we track, interpret, and utilize data. With these tools, you can automate your data collection and analysis process, providing real-time insights that can inform your decision-making. Here are a few no-code tools that can aid you in your data-tracking journey:

1. **Google Analytics:** This tool provides valuable insights about your website traffic, user behaviour, and engagement patterns. It enables you to track important metrics like page views, bounce rate, session duration, and conversion rate.

2. **Mixpanel**: Mixpanel provides an in-depth analysis of user interactions with your product. This tool is particularly useful for tracking events, funnels, and user journeys, providing insights into how customers

interact with your product over time. It also helps track retention, conversion, and churn rate, key indicators of your product's success.

3. **Typeform:** This no-code tool is a go-to for collecting qualitative data from your users through customized forms and surveys. It's a great way to gather customer feedback, learn more about user experiences, and collect suggestions for feature enhancements.

4. **Zapier:** Zapier acts as a bridge between different applications, facilitating the automation of tasks. For instance, you can set up a 'Zap' that automatically updates a Google Spreadsheet each time a user completes a Typeform survey on your website. This seamless integration saves you time and ensures that valuable customer feedback is never missed.

5. **Airtable:** Airtable is a versatile tool that operates as a hybrid between a spreadsheet and a database. It's incredibly useful for organizing, tracking, and visualizing data from various aspects of your business, including customer data, product roadmap, task management, and more.

6. **Google Data Studio:** Once you have your data collected and organized, Google Data Studio can help you visualize that data in comprehensive dashboards and reports. These visual aids can be particularly useful for spotting trends, making comparisons, and presenting your data to stakeholders.

These no-code tools, when combined effectively, can form a robust data tracking and analysis system, keeping you informed and agile in your decision-making process.

Looking beyond the numbers

While these tools can offer valuable insights, it's essential to remember that they are only as powerful as the interpretations you make from them. Data is not a magical solution in itself but a tool to guide your understanding and decision-making. It's crucial to consider the broader context of your business environment, the qualitative feedback from your users, and your intuitive understanding as a founder.

By focusing on actionable metrics rather than vanity metrics, you can obtain a more realistic picture of your business's health. It will keep you grounded, direct your focus to what truly matters, and guide your strategic decision-making. It's not always an easy path, and the truth may sometimes be less glamorous than the vanity metrics would suggest, but this approach is essential for driving sustainable growth.

In conclusion, tracking and analyzing metrics can be challenging, particularly when the results aren't as anticipated. Yet, this process remains a cornerstone of the product development journey, serving as a consistent reference throughout your business's evolution. Regardless of the insights your data provides, there's always a path forward. It might involve refining your concept, pivoting based on feedback, or charting the next phase of your product's growth. Always remember, every piece of data is a steppingstone towards your business's future.

12

The tech echo system

When I hear people talk about no-code tools, I think their immediate thoughts are of the app builders like Bubble, Webflow, and Glide. That may even stretch to the tools that join and automate processes, such as Zapier or Make. What is often overlooked is the vast array of tools and resources that allow you to ideate, build and grow a startup for a very small amount of money. Over the last couple of years, I've come to believe that no-code is much more than software. No-code can be employed as a mindset that can be applied to every aspect of your business, from financial management, to hiring and managing staff, to growth and investment, and everything else in between.

My no-code toolbox is vast and multifaceted, and leveraging these resources effectively can profoundly impact your startup's trajectory. Each component of this expansive ecosystem plays a crucial role in the ideation, development, and promotion of your product. Over the last couple of years I've gathered a collection of resources ranging from graphic and photo websites, through to startup accelerators and communities, to how to find additional people and money. The tech echo system is vast and growing, but below I have created my essential go-to's for everything you'll ever need on your no-code startup journey.

Tools to help build your product

Graphics and fonts

I often hear many entrepreneurs talking about their MVP not having to be perfect. That is absolutely true. I think if your app functions at the most basic level and it doesn't have all of the bells and whistles, then that's ok. However, I personally believe that there should be an element of care in your brand – even if there is a lot of room to grow. I remember when I was freelancing as a designer, I was asked to take a look at a one-page website that was not generating the response the owner thought it deserved. Taking one look at the Comic Sans font and the pixelated hero image didn't exactly scream professional. In less than ten minutes, I changed the font and the image and it looked a billion times better. A well-designed visual element can captivate your audience and set the tone for their experience. Free and premium sites like Vectorstock, Vecteezy, and Envato Elements are treasure troves of commercial-use graphics and fonts. These resources can infuse your app with a unique character, reinforcing its visual appeal. When using these resources, it's crucial to thoroughly review their licensing agreements. Some sites may require creator attribution, especially when utilizing their free resources. If you wish to modify these elements, vector editors like Adobe Illustrator or online tools such as Vecteezy's SVG editor offer easy-to-use interfaces. For non-designers, Canva provides a user-friendly platform to create bespoke graphics with its intuitive drag-and-drop functionality.

Photographs

It might seem obvious that I'm talking about using stock photos for your no-code app, but you'll be shocked at the number of founders I've encountered spending a few hundred pounds on a photo shoot of a man holding a phone or a cafe scene. High-quality photographs can significantly enhance your app's aesthetic and user experience. Stock photo sites such as iStockphoto, Pexels, and Unsplash offer a vast array of images spanning various themes and styles. But should you not find what you're looking for, don't underestimate the power of your smartphone camera. With the right framing and lighting, you can produce unique, tailor-made photographs that encapsulate your vision perfectly. I once ran an e-commerce store selling household goods to students. Rather than pay a tonne for a photographer, I used my dad's basic digital camera (before the days of smartphones), a white bed sheet pinned to a wall and an art lamp that cost £10. They weren't exactly Annie Leibovitz, but they got me the sales.

Videos

As one of the most engaging forms of content, videos can effectively communicate your message and bring your product to life. Stock video sites, including Envato Elements, offer a multitude of videos that can be customized to suit your narrative. However, if you prefer a more personalized touch, consider creating your own video content. Modern smartphones offer excellent video quality, and with inexpensive accessories such as a microphone and ring light, you can produce professional-grade videos that resonate with your audience. My entire video setup (apart from my mobile phone) cost me no more than £50.

Gig workers

There may come a time when you need expertise or skills that lie outside your purview, or when your time could be used better. This is where freelance platforms like Fiverr and Upwork come into play. These platforms can connect you with professionals across various fields, from video editing to complex programming tasks. Investing in these services can save you valuable time and ensure high-quality results, allowing you to focus on the broader aspects of your startup. I will often use Fiverr for small jobs like video editing or animation. In the early days I had a really complex Bubble workflow I just could not figure out. I paid a gig worker £15 to have it fixed within a couple of hours.

Project management

Efficient project management is the backbone of any successful startup. Tools like Trello, Asana, and Monday.com can help you organize your daily tasks and keep track of your long-term business roadmap. A particularly versatile tool in this category is Notion, an all-in-one workspace that facilitates writing, planning, collaboration, and organization. By integrating Notion with other tools such as Google Calendar, Typeform, and Email through Zapier, you can automate various processes, enhancing productivity and workflow efficiency. I plan out all of my database and page structures on Notion so I can check off each section as I build.

Copy

Years ago, I used to spend so much of my time trying to create the perfect copy for my apps and websites. I do love to write, but I often find that when I'm creating my own products, I just get too caught up with making it 'perfect' and spend countless and wasted hours on it. Thanks to the developments in AI, I now use tools like ChatGPT to craft my headlines and re-edit my web copy. This is the prompt I used to create the first headline on Willo.Social:

'You have created a private members community for adults with chronic health conditions. Membership offers exclusive deals and events in our member's local community. Imagine you are an expert copywriter in the field of health. Create an engaging and friendly H1 headline of no more than ten words that will encourage them to join.'

The response was:

'Your Supportive Circle: Deals and events for local health communities.'

Tools for raising money

Every startup inevitably encounters a crucial crossroads where one needs to determine whether to continue bootstrapping or seek external funding through angel investors or Venture Capitalists (VCs). Drawing from my personal experience, I can assure you that there's no universally correct choice; it's a decision that needs to be tailor-made, considering both personal circumstances and business needs.

In the past, I've been down both roads – bootstrapping and raising VC funds. When we decided to raise funds, it was because we were on the precipice of a significant growth phase. We had a burgeoning customer base interested in our product, and scaling our marketing operations to reach a wider audience required a substantial infusion of capital. Consequently, we decided to exchange about 20% of our business equity for the requisite funds.

This decision was a double-edged sword. On the positive side, we received a substantial cash boost that allowed us to expand our operations rapidly. On the flip side, it meant surrendering partial ownership of our company, a potential drawback depending on your perspective and long-term goals.

Truth be told, the aura around fundraising had a hypnotic effect on me, fueling the perception that raising money was a de facto step in qualifying as a 'legitimate' startup. In retrospect, I realize that my no-code mindset would have served me well in this situation, allowing me to consider other pathways to success. Several highly successful companies, like Mailchimp, SurveyMonkey, and Minecraft, were bootstrapped to profitability, demonstrating that raising external funding isn't a mandatory milestone on the road to success.

Regardless of the route you choose for your business, I've found that integrating no-code methodologies can significantly streamline and simplify the processes involved in either scenario.

The process of securing investment is gruelling and demands in-depth research. My approach starts early, delving into the investment landscape to identify potential connections.

Apollo: Apollo.io is an engagement and sales platform that I've leveraged to seek out investors and the companies they have invested in. This platform offers free credits that facilitate outreach to these key contacts. Since most investors prefer introductions through mutual connections, I make an effort to reach out to the founders of these companies. By creating automated outreach emails, I invite these individuals for a brief Zoom call to discuss their experiences and learn about their investor relationships. This method helps me cultivate connections that may eventually facilitate investor introductions.

Google Sheets: To stay organized, I create a database of VCs and their contacts using platforms like AngelList and Techcrunch for research. Some VCs are open to cold outreach, and I mark them accordingly. I integrate Google Sheets with Apollo using Zapier, enabling automatic account and task creation in Apollo whenever I add a new row to the sheet.

ChatGPT: To refine my pitch deck, I use ChatGPT to help polish my copy. I use plugins like Bing Search to quickly gather relevant industry facts. I also use ChatGPT to analyse successful pitch decks and summarize their key points, which I then incorporate into my own deck.

Gmail: With Zapier, I connect Gmail to Google Sheets to help me track responses. If specific search strings like 'investment pitch deck' appear in an email, it gets added to a new row in Google Sheets, maintaining a record of who is responding and their feedback.

Tools for managing your business with no-code

Sales is important to any business, whether you're backed by investors or your own savings. It's even more important for those businesses that want to be purely self-reliant on organic sales and growth. The goal is to streamline all routine tasks to focus on the ultimate objectives of driving sales and achieving profitability.

CRM

Customer Relationship Management (CRM) is instrumental in fostering strong relationships with your customers. Tools such as Hubspot, Monday, and Zoho CRM can streamline this process by managing customer interactions and automating tasks like follow-up emails for new leads. These tools not only enhance customer satisfaction but also free up time for you to focus on other critical areas of your business.

Social media

Google Alerts: I set up alerts on topics related to my product, including competitor activities. This helps me keep a pulse on industry developments and understand the type of content my competitors are producing.

ChatGPT: ChatGPT is a versatile tool that I use to generate ideas for social media content and write blog posts, which I can then schedule for automated publishing.

Canva: Despite being a designer myself, I find Canva an invaluable tool for rapidly creating captivating images for my social media posts, freeing up a significant chunk of my time.

Social Media Scheduler: Tools like Social Pilot or Sprout Social allow me to automate my social media posts. I can set up a content calendar and have my posts pre-scheduled for the coming weeks, ensuring consistency in my social media presence.

Sales

Apollo.io: Apollo comes in handy in the sales arena too. It allows me to create automated email sequences for potential customers. I utilize their LinkedIn Chrome Extension to discover potential customers and add them to the email sequence with just a few clicks.

Calendly: Calendly is a scheduling tool that integrates with Google or Microsoft Calendars. It makes it straightforward for a potential customer to pick an available slot in my schedule and book a meeting instantly. I make sure to add a Calendly link to all of my outbound emails for seamless scheduling.

ChatGPT: I use ChatGPT to generate the content for my email outreach and to brainstorm engaging email subjects. Interestingly, I've observed a higher success rate with emails crafted by AI compared to those I've written myself.

Trello: Trello is a Kanban board tool that helps me organize tasks and move them between boards based on progress. I use Trello to track all my pending tasks. I've previously connected Gmail to Trello so customer messages automatically generate a new task on my Trello board. One of my favourite boards is the 'Opportunities' board, where I collate information about startup competitions, grant applications, or VC pitching opportunities, ensuring I never miss a potential growth opportunity.

Google Workspace: I extensively use Google Workspace, especially Gmail, Drive, and Calendar. Their seamless integration and cloud-based structure allow me to access all my documents from anywhere in the world across all my devices.

Accounting software: Arguably, the least exciting but absolutely vital part of any no-code toolbox is reliable accounting software. Most accounting software can directly connect to your bank account, providing real-time visibility into your financial performance. This overview allows me to monitor my expenditure and keep a tight grip on my bootstrapped finances.

Accelerators

Tech accelerators have become a critical component in the startup ecosystem, providing a conducive environment for budding entrepreneurs to nurture their ideas and grow their businesses. Broadly speaking, a tech accelerator is a fixed-term, cohort-based program that includes mentorship and educational components and often culminates in a public pitch event or demo day. These programs provide a structure for startups to gain traction, build a robust network, receive mentorship, and possibly secure investment.

Some of the world's most renowned accelerators include Y Combinator, TechStars, and 500 Startups, which have a long history of successful exits and unicorns among their alumni. However, the reach of these accelerators extends beyond the major tech hubs. Most local business ecosystems offer some form of an accelerator program to stimulate economic growth and encourage innovation within their communities.

In recent years, as no-code development tools have gained popularity, accelerators have adapted to this trend by offering dedicated workshops and programs to support no-code startups. These programs focus on leveraging the power of no-code tools to build products efficiently and leanly.

I've had the privilege of participating in three major accelerators throughout my entrepreneurial journey. Interestingly, I attended the same accelerator twice, with a four-year gap in between. My experiences in both instances were starkly different, highlighting the shifting landscape of the tech startup world.

During my first stint, the emphasis was on finding a tech co-founder – someone proficient in coding. This proved to be a challenging endeavour, particularly for those of us who lacked connections within the tech community. Fast forward four years and the approach has drastically changed. Lean startup methodology took centre stage, with no-code tools being highlighted as essential resources for rapid product development. The accelerator even dedicated an entire day to a no-code hackathon, providing us with a hands-on learning experience about various no-code tools.

These accelerators were instrumental in my entrepreneurial journey. The structured environment allowed for exploration, learning, and mistakes in a safe, supportive setting. Perhaps the most invaluable aspect of these accelerators was the access to mentors and industry experts. Their guidance helped us refine our product ideas and navigate common hurdles, providing us with insights that would have been difficult to acquire independently.

However, it's important to remember that while accelerators can be a useful springboard, they are not a prerequisite for startup success. Many unicorns and successful startups have been built outside of accelerator programs. What's crucial is the entrepreneur's vision, determination, and ability to adapt and learn.

If you are considering an accelerator, here are a few tips:

- **Research**: Not all accelerators are created equal. Do your research to find an accelerator that aligns with your startup's mission and goals. Look at their track record, mentorship pool, and the experiences of past participants.

- **Prepare:** Most accelerators have a competitive application process. Spend time refining your application and pitch. Clearly articulate your business idea, market opportunity, and why your team is the one to execute it.

- **Engage:** If accepted, take full advantage of the resources provided. Actively engage with mentors, attend workshops, and network with your cohort.

Ultimately, participating in an accelerator is an investment in your startup's future. Whether it's gaining mentorship, building your network, or learning to leverage no-code tools, the experience can provide you with the tools and knowledge to navigate your entrepreneurial journey.

A note about team members

As well as the physical tools and communities aimed at helping you on your journey, another important resource is people. I see many founders talking about co-founders and building a team, so I wanted to share with you how I approach the subject.

No-code tools have fundamentally revolutionized my approach to conducting business. However, the implications of no-code extend far beyond mere drag-and-drop builders; it instils a mindset and establishes a framework for lean operations and efficient resource allocation. Reflecting on my journey, I can see that adopting this no-code mindset has transformed not only my product development approach but also the way I manage and structure my teams.

In the not-so-distant past, I found myself following a 'traditional' path of startup evolution. I would initiate my projects with cost-effective no-code tools, but once the product began to take shape, I felt compelled to replicate the conventional startup model. This model often involved heavy investment in team expansion, aggressive marketing, office spaces, and a host of other elements, most of which were influenced more by external perceptions than internal necessities.

One could attribute this rush towards conforming to the startup stereotype to a sense of FOMO (fear of missing out). I often found myself comparing my journey to that of other startups, most of whom had secured substantial funding and had a proven business model. Yet, I was being swept along by this wave of comparison, often making decisions detrimental to my venture.

A clear example of this was a previous venture where I hurried into choosing a co-founder, only to realize later that our visions and working styles weren't aligned. We were then quick to onboard people for roles that, in hindsight, were unnecessary. The no-code mindset, had I applied it during those crucial decision-making periods, would have resulted in vastly different outcomes.

Here's how adopting a no-code mindset could have reshaped those decisions:

- **Self-reliance:** With the tools and capabilities offered by no-code, I could have built the startup on my own, at least until I found the right person to share the co-founder role. No-code empowers solo entrepreneurs to validate their ideas and build a minimum viable product without the immediate need for a team.

- **Automation:** A significant advantage of no-code tools is the degree of automation they facilitate. Many tasks traditionally requiring human intervention can be automated using no-code, making several roles redundant. This automation not only saves costs but also increases efficiency and reduces the likelihood of errors.

- **Reduced dependence on developers:** No-code tools eliminate the need for a traditional developer to build the product. This not only saves considerable resources but also allows for more control and agility in product development, with the ability to make changes on the fly without waiting for the developer's availability.

The essence of no-code lies in maximizing impact with minimal resources. It instils a decision-making framework where every choice is predicated on its ability to validate an assumption in the least time-consuming and resource-intensive manner.

Having a co-founder and a team can be a tremendous asset when the synergy works. If you're reading this and already have a team or a co-founder in place, it's not cause for panic. Instead, it's an opportunity to incorporate the principles of no-code in your decision-making process henceforth.

On the flip side, if you're a solo founder, the no-code approach is an affirmation that you're on the right track. Resist the urge to rush into decisions because they fit the 'typical startup' narrative. Adopt the 'no-code' approach – validate the need for additional resources or team members before making the commitment. This no-code mindset will not only save you resources but also enhance your startup's agility and resilience.

13

Conversations with founders

Today, the rise of no-code tools has paved the way for a plethora of innovative businesses. A standout example is Makerpad, a no-code educational platform built using no-code itself! Impressively, while raking in over $200,000 annually in sales, it caught the attention of Zapier, which acquired it for an undisclosed sum. This trend has empowered non-technical founders to embrace no-code solutions in launching their ventures. I had the privilege of conversing with three such founders who are making remarkable strides in their respective domains.

Jof Walters: Million Labs and Seesy

Jof Walters stands at the helm of Million Labs, a renowned no-code agency. His enterprise is dedicated to assisting founders in the ideation and construction of startups using the powerful no-code tool Bubble. With the capacity to support over 100 founders every month, Jof's expertise in the no-code domain has flourished. However, his involvement extends beyond just expertise; he has also ventured into the world of investment.

One of the remarkable developments under Million Labs' banner, which also attracted Jof's investment, is a startup named Seesy. This innovative venture, the brainchild of Adam Corbett, offers a platform for video CV creation. Within a mere six weeks of its product being built, Seesy attracted a staggering six-figure investment from external sources.

Tell me about your background and how you arrived at no-code.

My background is a more salubrious sort of environment. I spent 20 years in banking and ended up in the Challenger banking community in 2015, and I got out of that in 2018. I thought, well, what am I going to do now? And actually, I'd had an idea that I wanted to pursue, and I'd tried to build it myself. I'm not that technical; I am a traditional non-technical founder. So, I decided I'd build it with this new no-code stuff. Simon, who's the co-founder of Million Labs, pointed me towards Bubble. We used Bubble to build it, and it didn't work. It was an idea that didn't take off. But actually, that didn't matter because what we figured out was we'd spent some hours and a tiny bit of money, a couple of $1,000, next to nothing to prove that. That became the kernel of Million Labs, saving money and testing ideas that otherwise we would have spent a quarter of a million pounds on.

How does Million Labs help founders?

We help around 100 startups every month from all over the world, founded by all sorts of people. Some we invest in, and some pay the agency team to build their ideas. Million Labs is a high-volume idea-testing platform today. That's what we're really about, and in the process, we hope to find and back the winners. When it comes to ideas, 40 people can have the same good idea, and only one of them will turn into a massive business.

Bubble has a fairly high learning curve. How did you find it as a complete beginner?

That's an interesting question. I did a lot of courses. The mistake a lot of founders make is that they leap straight to

Bubble because it's a really good platform in terms of its flexibility. If you want to build a running app and stick it on an Apple Watch, you can do that with Bubble. If you want to build a forecasting engine for crypto balance sheets, you can do it with Bubble. So, it's incredibly flexible. But as you say, that high learning curve means that often what we see is sort of that traditional founder behaviour of getting buried in the tech. They get lost in the making, and they forget that the most important thing to do is the testing. And so actually Glide and even Carrd, which is the most basic thing on Earth, you can use that to put a proposition on a page and send it out to a bunch of people and say and see if they're going to click a button to say, I'm interested.

So, would you recommend that founders new to no-code should take it a few steps back?

Yes. Today we use a lot of intermediary steps to do landing page tests and small functional tests that don't require something like Bubble. We're now seeing developments in the no-code space where they have iterated on what Bubble has done. Now we have a third generation of platforms coming that are as flexible as Bubble but are using things like AI to do the bits that people find the most difficult. A good example of this would be Appreggio.

Do you encounter many founders who want to build their ideas without first validating the problem through customer conversations?

I would categorize that in percentage terms as everybody, every single person. It's so rare that somebody has gone away and validated customer demand. And that's our main test for investment. We will push people back and say, 'go away and show me the 200 people that want this', or 'show me that you've got a big social following of people that have the same problem'.

I think no-code makes it so easy to jump straight into the building before doing any groundwork.

It does. I think that's an interesting point. The failure rate for no-code startups is very high because it's easy come, easy go. It's easier than it ever has been to make a new product. If I can make it and it doesn't immediately catch fire, I can give up.

Tell me more about Seesy because that is an interesting story. You went from building a Bubble product to getting investment in six weeks.

That's an interesting one. It was started by a gentleman named Adam, who is incredibly entrepreneurial. During the first Covid lockdown, he had a familiar problem of supporting staff through furlough. His original proposition was to create something that would follow the furlough scheme and de-risk employment. While he was doing that, he got really interested in the fact that it was really easy to record videos on a smartphone. Video CV's seemed like a really interesting space to go into and nobody was doing it at the time.

What was the first version like?

It was essentially a video capture component attached to a database of jobs and employees. It wasn't complicated and so that took no time at all to build; literally 20 hours.

Incredible. Enough to prove the concept in order to get additional funding?

Absolutely. Since funding, the technology has moved on a lot. What made it successful was the founder using his network to push the concept really quickly. The MVP was able to demonstrate simply that there was a demand for the product and that is the most important part. It's enough to get the interest of an investor. Unfortunately, what we see more commonly is somebody that has no evidence and no traction.

How has the reaction been from investors when it comes to no-code MVPs?

No-code is a lot more understood now. When we first started, the general pushback that we received was, 'Oh, you don't own your IP'. That thinking is out of date now. There have been a handful of no-code startups that have been really successful and a lot more that have been successful enough that no-code has become an accepted route to market.

What are you most excited about when it comes to the future of no-code?

No-code is just getting going. It's exciting to see how this technology is democratizing product development and investment. I'm a 46-year-old white British male and I was really fortunate to be born in the place and time that I was. The thing that I like about no-code is that the people that I see building startups now don't look like me, they did not go to university, and they're not in a first-world country. We're seeing people build technology businesses that focus on problems that are relevant to them. These might be small businesses that are making it easier to book space in warehouses or to book an appointment with a doctor. They may never become unicorns, but these are the type of companies that drive and grow an economy. That is what excites me. Plus, all the new developments are making product building easier, like AI tools.

You're a Bubble fan, but what other no-code tools do you use regularly?

Interestingly, the most commonly used things within Million Labs would not necessarily be perceived as no-code tools. Stripe is the second most popular thing we use. Everything we do is also enabled by a variety of Google products and API's.

What advice would you give to a no-code founder who's got absolutely no experience? What would you say are the most important things that they should do to create a successful no-code startup?

Go and find a real group of people that have the problem that you're trying to solve and really sit with them. Don't show them your idea. Measure the problem they've got and see how much pain they're actually going through. Those early relationships are really important. If you can find five people that share the same problem, that will supercharge your startup. The data that you get out of those five relationships will absolutely fundamentally change your business.

Stephen Mitchell: SQCDP

Steve Mitchell is a former engineering manager who founded SQCDP (Safety, Quality, Cost, Delivery, and People) in 2022. SQCDP helps manufacturers measure and respond to how they are performing against a series of common indicators.

Tell me about how you discovered the initial problem that SQCDP solves.

My background is in engineering management, and I've worked with everything from small independent companies right through to big corporates like Coca-Cola. I was working for a large government-based organization, and I'd been there for two years. It was a frustrating environment because I had this SQCDP system of whiteboards and paperwork, which was collecting all of the daily data from the operators, and then providing handovers to team leaders. They were just printed form templates that had to be updated with a red or green pen every shift. With 15 shifts per week, that was 45 data points to add. After a month, there were these huge swathes of red dots and green dots, and nobody could really follow.

As the engineering manager, I was finding that every time we had a review of production performance, problems were always being placed at the hands of engineering or maintenance. It was unsettling, and I knew there was something not quite right. So, I started to record and track the data on a spreadsheet.

Within a few weeks, I was able to see where exactly the problems lay, and we were able to implement processes. Because everything was normally done on paper, there were always big gaps in data. For example, we were supposed to manufacture 500 parts, yet we've only produced 200. Production reports that there was a 30-minute breakdown at the start of the shift, so on paper, it's assumed that is the problem. Yet, 30 minutes of downtime only accounts for 40 parts not being produced, so what happened to the rest? What part of the production line is not working?

How did you get from that MVP spreadsheet to a technical product the whole team could use?

I knew that there were no-code app builders out there. At the time, I felt that I was in the line of fire at work, so I'm going to fix this for me. If it helps the business then that's great, but I wanted to make sure that myself and my team were protected.

What were your first steps in building a solution?

I researched different no-code builders that were on the market. I tried one that was like a web-based access database and found it to be a bit clunky for what I needed, and it wasn't going to give me the output that I needed. What I wanted was data to be captured on a terminal and then have that data updated in real time. It had to follow the SQCDP theme of our we safe? Are we making the product the right quality? Do we understand our downtimes and where we're losing time? And are we understanding where we're underperforming?

Which tool did you use for this?

I came across Glide. It was early in its development, but I joined its growing community. I could already see that with the basic tools that were in there, I could apply the small parts of database logic that I already knew. If I encountered a problem, I could search the web or turn to the community for help.

As a non-technical founder, how did you stay motivated to complete your app when things became a little trickier?

I took really simple steps, but I knew that if I kept going, I would get the outcome that I wanted. Plus, I had a real fire for the problem, and I was so annoyed that it wasn't already in use. It felt like it was on me to solve this problem finally. I worked every morning on the build for about an hour in a coffee shop before I had to go to work. I did that for about six months. I would work on one part at a time which I think gave me the satisfaction that I'd achieved something. It gave me the confidence to go and move on to the next one.

What was the hardest part of the build for you?

I encountered some problems with the database calculations that would give me the right figures. Then I would ask myself, 'What's the best way to display this on a chart?' I had only ever seen the data displayed in a written form, so that was when I hit a small stumbling block. I ended up using Quick Charts, which would push and pull the data between itself and my app. It was just about doing some research and looking in the right places to find the correct module, community member, or guide to get the help that I needed.

How did your employer react to this game-changing solution that you created?

I had to break it down for them as they were concerned about security, particularly as it's government based. We had to take some delicate steps and coach them through what Glide was and how data was stored. Ultimately, the head of information security for the entire European network said, yes, I love it; I'm happy.

How did it feel to let people try it for the first time?

We ran it across a two-week trial period, which meant there were 30 shifts worth of people. I was nervous, thinking I hope they don't break it, especially as it went very quiet right after I handed it over. It turned out they were just really happy with the app and were finding it really easy. I was afraid they would be very against it because, essentially, it would be showing them where they were going wrong, but it was the complete opposite reaction. At the end of the two-week trial, the results showed that production performance had gone up by 15% and quality increased by 5%. It also prevented the company from needing an overtime weekend to recover underperformance, and the overall cost saving was £85,000.

You must have felt a real sense of elation to see it doing so well.

Yes, incredibly elated. It was that affirmation that I was on the right path.

SQCDP is now a startup in its own right. How did you transition from the trial to where you are now?

Unfortunately, the trial could not go beyond two weeks due to the nature of the organization. They required passwords to be removed and major changes to be made, which were just not possible. It was incredibly disappointing. I ended up moving to another company where I discovered the same problem existed. It was then that it dawned on me that I could have used this product at all of my previous jobs and that this was a product in its own right. If it could solve the problem there, could it solve the problem at other manufacturing facilities also? That was when it started me on the journey of exploring and asking whether this could be a business.

Did you join an accelerator at the start of your journey? How did that help you?

I spent six months on an accelerator programme, validating how my no-code product can be useful to other customers. What features are people using? Are they all using it the same way? What aspect of it is going to make the customer pay?

We also completed a no-code workshop that had integrations into AI. That is an exciting next step for me and my product, as AI will be able to show managers what they need to do rather than just showing charts. I'm able to do that with no-code and that's very exciting. I can now be creative again and take my product to the next level.

Why do you think no-code is so important in today's world?

If no-code did not exist I would have had to knock on the doors of professional agencies. I'd have to tell them what I want to achieve and for them to interpret what they think I need. That would have been frustrating and costly. No-code offered something that I needed; a simple solution. It's creating an organic and fair environment for people like me.

What would your advice be to somebody who's in a similar situation where they've got no experience with building products but have a great idea?

First, narrow your problem because there were times when I was trying to build everything and kept going off on a tangent. Second, find a no-code builder that suits them and their skill set. Maybe you don't like the interface or how rigid a theme is. Maybe you want something with an in-built database, etc. Remove any fiction before you start because then you're more likely to succeed. There are so many tools to choose from that you will find one that really feels natural to you. I also tell people to read the guides before they start and get involved with the communities if they have one. The no-code community is very supportive and there is always someone there who has experienced or solved any issues you too might be facing.

Michael John Magdongon: Strabo

Michael is the founder of Strabo, a customizable dashboard that lets users manage their global financial portfolio. They recently raised almost a quarter of a million pounds on the investment platform, Seedrs.

Thank you for joining me in the conversation about no-code.

Thank you. It was never my intention to pursue a brand or presence in the no-code industry per se. It was convenient. No-code was a means to an end. But the more I got into it, the more I loved it. I loved the application, especially what it could do, not only for non-technical founders but even for people who are on a budget or need to or want to roll something out quickly. It's been a great experience, and I've been having fun being part of the community.

Tell me a bit about your background before you became a no-code founder.

I'm a non-technical founder. I'm a two-time founder of a small business in Chicago, so I have more of a business background. I did that for about four and a half years and did my MBA abroad. During that time, I worked in venture capital, and then from there I worked at a big tech firm over at Amazon, primarily in operations management. I did that for a few years, but by then the entrepreneurship bug was scratching. I left to pursue Strabo, which is a fintech application that helps expats manage their assets across the world.

How did you initially come up with the problem?

I'm an American who lives here in London, and I have accounts and assets in the States as well as over the globe. I'm constantly moving money from point A to point B. So, in addition to that and the ambiguity of where I will retire, it became increasingly difficult how to plan for the future and generate wealth and plan for retirement. So that's where the idea of Strabo came into fruition. I searched the market, but

I couldn't really find anything that fit my needs. So, I think it was at a great time when I wanted to start a company. I was ready for the next stage of my career. I sat with it; did the interviews, and user discovery. I went through the full research process and then finally made the decision to pursue Strabo full-time.

You chose Bubble are your no-code platform. How did you choose that as the foundation of your product?

The first year of starting the company was just a learning experience. And the way that we approach product development was in a very traditional way. We hired a developer, we used a typical tech stack, and ywe paid for AWS, etc. That created a problem. Number one, it's expensive. Number two, it takes a long time. And number three, finding a developer, a good one that's going to do it within budget is also really challenging. We did find one and he was really good, but it just didn't work out. After that we found another developer, but he wasn't so good. We then found a third developer who also wasn't very good. It just became absolutely challenging and expensive to keep finding and replacing people. Plus, at the end of the day, what we really need to do is roll out a product so we could get further validation and testing. That's when I started exploring no-code. I knew about it, but I was stuck in my old ways of thinking. I thought a product had to be built a certain way.

But I'm glad we went the direction of no-code because we were able to build a product in a very quick time, under budget, and we got some users actually using the application. I went through the pain points of doing things the traditional way, which then led me to do things in untraditional way.

And how long did it take you to build from start to finish?

Two and a half months.

That's amazing. What has been the response to the product?

Very positive. Really positive. We got some really good feedback from investors and from our user base. From there, we were able to raise capital. We were then able to hire a CTO (Chief Technology Officer) who suggested that the time was right to move to a traditional tech stack. We're relaunching our application, but we still have the Bubble application. We're thinking of using that as a testing vehicle because we're able to build something really quick, get it out there, and have people using an actual application.

When you were raising money and you informed investors that you've got a no-code product, what was their reaction?

That was interesting because, in the early days of starting this company, we received advice that investors don't look highly on no-code solutions. But when we've been pitching it, only one or two looked down on it. But for the vast majority, it didn't matter. We'd got something to market and validated our ideas. Raising capital would then allow us to transition to normal tech stacking. Why spend a lot of valuable time and money building something that people don't want when you could just do it with no-code? And even if it's still a sizable investment, it's still nowhere near the cost of what it would have taken to build something else.

Do you use no-code in any other way, such as managing the business?

Right now, our website is still on no-code. We're using Webflow for our main landing page, and then the application is just a normal tech stack. We use tools like Notion and Airtable pretty much day-to-day for tracking tasks and managing our activities.

What advice would you give to a first-time no-code founder?

I think the best piece of advice is when you're starting a business, especially a tech business, you're not really starting a business. You're starting a series of experiments. Experiment first, then when you get it right, that's when it turns into a business. So don't look at it as you're starting a company; look at it as if you're starting a series of experiments that you're trying to validate. I think that will remove a lot of the unnecessary things you think you have to do from your day-to-day tasks. Then you can just focus on the things that really matter, which is really just getting validation on every piece of your business.

Resources

There is a growing collection of resources available for no-code founders; from chatbots, chart makers, API directories, design tools, and AI. To help you on your way, I have assembled a collection of no-code tools and resources that you can use in your own startup. This list isn't exhaustive, but you can find an up-to-date collection at https://nocodestartup.co

Remember to tag your no-code builds with #nocodestartupbook to be featured on our website.

AI

ChatGPT	Conversational AI tool	http://chat.openai.com
Bard	Conversational AI by Google	https://bard.google.com/
Blits	An AI-driven conversational ecosystem	www.blits.ai/
Levity	Automate everyday tasks with AI	https://levity.ai/
Metatext	Build, annotate and manage NLP products	https://metatext.ai/
Obviously AI	A no-code data science tool	www.obviously.ai/

APIs

Backendless	Complete API development	https://backendless.com/
BaseQL	Create a simple API or a full-fledged Backend from existing Airtable	www.baseql.com/
Rapid API	Search and connect to thousands of API's	https://rapidapi.com/hub

App builders

Adalo	Create interactive apps with customizable templates and components	www.adalo.com/
Appeggio	Appeggio lets you create powerful apps across the web and mobile	https://appeggio.com/
Apphive	No-code mobile app builder	https://apphive.io/
AppMatser.io	Mobile app builder with a powerful backend	https://appmaster.io/
Appsheet	Build powerful apps using Google Sheets	https://about.appsheet.com/
Betty Blocks	Build low code business applications	www.bettyblocks.com/
Bravo Studio	Native mobile apps powered with AI	www.bravostudio.app/
Clappia	Build digital transformational apps	www.clappia.com/
Fliplet	Build mobile and web apps without code	https://fliplet.com/
Flutterflow	A powerful platform for building apps	hhttps://flutterflow.io/
Kodika.io	Create iOS and Android apps with drag and drop	https://kodika.io/
Microsoft Power Apps	No-code apps for business	https://powerapps.microsoft.com/
Moxly	AI app builder for iOS and Android	www.moxly.io/
PandaSuite	A flexible no-code tool for building apps and presentations	https://pandasuite.com/
Sandbox Commerce	Turn your e-commerce store into a mobile app	www.sandboxcommerce.com/
Thunkable	No-code mobile app development	https://thunkable.com/#/

Automation

airSlate	Create document workflows	www.airslate.com/
Boomi	Powerful business automations	https://boomi.com/
Flowshot.ai	Apply AI to your Google Sheets	http://flowshot.ai/
Goodflow	Automate and manage business workflows	https://goodflow.io/
Hipporello	Supercharge your Trello boards	www.hipporello.com/
Make.com	Powerful visual automation	www.make.com/en
Jestor	All-in-one workflow automation	https://jestor.com/
Jotform Sign	Signature automation tool	www.jotform.com/ products/sign/
Parabola	Automate complex workflows	https://parabola.io/
Scribe	Create visual step-by-step guides	https://scribehow. com/
Tango	Capture and automate processes in seconds	www.tango.us/
Twilio	Automated customer engagement	www.twilio.com
Zapier	Connect thousands of apps with ease	https://zapier.com/

Blockchain

Mash	Micropayments with Bitcoin	https://mash.com/
ICME	Build Web3 apps without code	www.icme.io/
Abridged	Build and manage decentralized projects	https://abridged.io/
Niftify	Create an NFT business in seconds	www.niftify.io/

Charts

Graphy	Create visual graphs from your data	https://graphy.app/
Hadmean	Create admin apps in seconds	https://hadmean.com/
Image Charts	Instantly create beautiful charts	www.image-charts.com/
Quickchart	Open Source chart API	https://quickchart.io/

Chatbots

BigRadar	Create no-code conversational chatbots	https://bigradar.io/
Blits.ai	A conversational AI ecosystem	www.blits.ai/
Botmother	Build chatbots without code	https://botmother.com/
Chatbot	Automize customer service chatbots	www.chatbot.com/
FlowXO	Premier AI chatbot tool	https://flowxo.com/
Formito	A chatbot that replaces basic forms	https://formito.com/
Joonbot	A no-code chatbot builder	https://joonbot.com/
Landbot	A powerful no-code chatbot builder	https://landbot.io/

Communities

Threado	A community management platform	www.threado.com/
Circle	A full community building and management tool	https://circle.so/
Discord	Create a dedicated community discussion platform	https://discord.com/

| Buddypress | Build versatile communities with this Wordpress Plugin | https://buddypress.org/ |
| MeltingSpot | Build an online community for any business | www.meltingspot.io/ |

Databases

Airtable	Build powerful databases with the simplicity of a spreadsheet	https://airtable.com/
Baserow	An open-source no-code database	https://baserow.io/
Google Sheets	Online spreadsheet that doubles as a database	www.google.co.uk/sheets/
Formbeaver	Build and host custom databases without code	www.formbeaver.com/
Jotform Tables	Collect and manage data in an all-in-one workspace	www.jotform.com/products/tables/
MicroDB	A no-code database with auto-generates screens	www.microdb.co/
Notion	A place to document and run your entire business	www.notion.so/

Design

Bootstrap Studio	A desktop app for building responsive websites	https://bootstrapstudio.io/
fffuel	Generate SVG files, patterns, and backgrounds in seconds	https://fffuel.co/
Studio	AI powered web design	https://studio.design/
Visily	Create stunning wireframes and prototypes	www.visily.ai/
Figma	A collaborative software for interface design	www.figma.com/

Canva	Create beautiful designs with a drag and drop interface	www.canva.com/en_gb/
Envato Elements	Download unlimited creative assets for your projects	https://elements.envato.com/
Vecteezy	Royalty free vector art, photos, and video	www.vecteezy.com/
Vectorstock	Get professional design assets for your business	www.vectorstock.com/

Digital downloads

Gumroad	Sell anything online through your own website	https://gumroad.com/
Payhip	A platform to sell digital courses and downloads	https://payhip.com/
Podia	Sell digital products, workshops, and courses	www.podia.com/

Ecommerce

Big Commerce	Professional e-commerce management platform	www.bigcommerce.co.uk/
Checkout Page	Embedded checkouts for your website	https://checkoutpage.co/
Maker	Turn Figma designs into store pages	www.maker.co/
Microweber	Create beautiful websites and Ecommerce stores	https://microweber.com/
Shopify	A global Ecommerce platform	www.shopify.com/
Wix	Build an Ecommerce store with easy drag and drop tools	https://wix.com

Email

Mailchimp	Cultivate and manage mailing lists	https://mailchimp.com/
Convertkit	A comprehensive email marketing tool	https://convertkit.com/
Aweber	Connect and automate email experiences	www.aweber.com/
Apollo	Create automated emails for buyers across the globe	www.apollo.io/

Forms

Cognito Forms	Build powerful forms easily	www.cognitoforms.com/
Flexform	Create flexible forms for your business	www.flexforms.com/
Jotform	Powerful forms with conditional logic	www.jotform.com/
MightyForms	Forms that collect payments	www.mightyforms.com/
Typeform	Build powerful forms that gather data	www.typeform.com

Games

Buildbox	Make games using AI	https://signup.buildbox.com/
Construct	Create browser-based games	www.construct.net/en
Gamesalad	Powerful no-code game maker	https://gamesalad.com/
GDevelop	A 2D/3D no-code game making app	https://gdevelop.io/
Stencyl	Create games without code	www.stencyl.com/

Landing pages

Bouncepage	Create mobile-friendly landing pages	https://bounce.page/
Bowwe	Create stunning websites and landing pages quickly	https://bowwe.com/
Builder	Create beautiful apps without code	www.builder.ai/
EarlyBird	Create simple landing pages that get customers	https://earlybird.im/
Grapedrop	A page builder for a variety of use cases	https://grapedrop.com/
Carrd	Simple, free, responsive landing pages	https://carrd.co/

Marketplaces

Kreezalid	Create and grow an online marketplace in minutes	www.kreezalid.com/
Sharetribe	Build an online marketplace quickly	www.sharetribe.com/
Tangram	A webflow powered marketplace	www.tangram.co/

Memberships

Ghost	Turn your audience into a business	https://ghost.org/
Memberspace	Launch a membership site in minutes	www.memberspace.com/
Wordpress	A versatile CMS that offers membership plugins	https://wordpress.org

Voice

Castup	AI-powered podcast creation tool	www.usecastup.com/
Descript	Powerful video and podcasting creation tool	www.descript.com/

| Otter | Get AI-generated notes from your meetings | https://otter.ai/ |
| Voiceflow | Design, test and launch voice assistants | www.voiceflow.com/ |

Web apps

Adalo	Build web apps without code with customizable templates and components	www.adalo.com/
AppGyver	Build apps visually	www.appgyver.com/
Beezer	Drag and drop progressive app builder	www.beezer.com/
Bubble	A powerful app building tool	https://bubble.io/
Caspio	Build powerful business applications	www.caspio.com/
Fliplet	Build web and mobile apps without code	https://fliplet.com/
Frontly	Build apps with AI in seconds	www.frontlyapp.com/
Glide	Create powerful business apps from your data	www.glideapps.com/
Glowbom	Build games and apps for popular platforms	https://glowbom.com/
Noodl	Create scalable low-code apps with AI	www.noodl.net/
Notaku	Notion powered websites	https://notaku.so/
Pory.io	A multi-purpose no-code app builder	https://pory.io/
Softr	Build software from a Google Sheet or Airtable	www.softr.io/
Stacker	Create high-impact apps from your business data	www.stackerhq.com/
Toddle	Create beautiful interfaces for your data	https://toddle.dev/
Typedream	Everything you need to be able to sell online	https://typedream.com/

| Wappler | A low-code tool for building responsive websites | https://wappler.io/ |
| Ycode | Create data-driven websites with beautiful designs | www.ycode.com/ |

Database field types

Text: Used to store any form of text data. This could include names, descriptions, addresses, and so on.

Long text: Similar to text but designed for larger bodies of text. Useful for storing comments, notes, or any other large text-based content.

Number: Used to store numerical data. This could be an integer or decimal and is often used for quantities, prices, or other numerical values.

Boolean: Used to store true/false or yes/no values. Can be useful for flags or indicators.

Date/time: Used to store a specific date and time. Useful for scheduling events, logging timestamps, etc.

Date: Used to store a date without a time component.

Time: Used to store a time without a date component.

Percentage: Used to store percentage values.

Currency: Used to store monetary values. The actual currency (like USD, EUR, etc.) can often be specified as well.

Email: Used to store email addresses. Some systems might automatically validate the data to ensure it's a properly formatted email address.

Phone number: Used to store phone numbers. Like email, some systems might validate the data.

URL: Used to store web URLs. Again, some systems might validate the data.

Image: Used to store image files.

File: Used to store any type of file.

List: Used to store a list of values. The values might be of any other type, like text or number.

Map: Used to store geographic locations.

Rating: Used to store rating values, such as a star rating out of five.

Colour: Used to store colour values, often in a format like hexadecimal.

Reference: Used to create a relationship between records in different tables. This is similar to a foreign key in a traditional relational database.

Common database operations

Here are a few common types of operations you might want to perform in a no-code database and the general formula you'd use for each one. These are simplified expressions, and the exact syntax or method you'd use could vary depending on the no-code platform you're using.

Basic arithmetic operations

- Addition: Field1 + Field2
- Subtraction: Field1 – Field2
- Multiplication: Field1 * Field2
- Division: Field1 / Field2
- Percentage: (Field1 / Field2) * 100
- Average: (Field1 + Field2 + ... + FieldN) / N

Text concatenation

- Joining two fields: Field1 & " " & Field2 (This would join Field1 and Field2 with a space in between.)

- Joining a field with a constant string: Field1 & "constant string"

Conditional operations

- If-Then-Else: If(Condition, Value_if_true, Value_if_false). This would return Value_if_true if the Condition is true, and Value_if_false if the Condition is false.

Date and time operations

- Difference between two dates: DateField1 – DateField2. This would typically give the difference in days.

- Extracting parts of a date: Functions like Year(DateField), Month(DateField), and Day(DateField) would give you the year, month, and day from a date field, respectively.

Aggregation functions

- Sum: Sum(FieldName) would give you the total sum of all values in FieldName.

- Count: Count(FieldName) would give you the number of records where FieldName is not null.

- Average: Average(FieldName) would give you the average value of FieldName.

- Min/Max: Min(FieldName) and Max(FieldName) would give you the smallest and largest value in FieldName, respectively.

Index

A quick word from Practical Inspiration Publishing...

We hope you found this book both practical and inspiring – that's what we aim for with every book we publish.

We publish titles on topics ranging from leadership, entrepreneurship, HR and marketing to self-development and wellbeing.

Find details of all our books at: www.practicalinspiration.com

 Did you know...

We can offer discounts on bulk sales of all our titles – ideal if you want to use them for training purposes, corporate giveaways or simply because you feel these ideas deserve to be shared with your network.

We can even produce bespoke versions of our books, for example with your organization's logo and/or a tailored foreword.

To discuss further, contact us on info@practicalinspiration.com.

 Got an idea for a business book?

We may be able to help. Find out more about publishing in partnership with us at: bit.ly/PIpublishing.

Follow us on social media...

 @PIPTalking

@pip_talking

@practicalinspiration

@piptalking

Practical Inspiration Publishing